A Marvelous Ministry

How the All-round Ministry of C H Spurgeon
Speaks to Us Today

by

Tim Curnow
Erroll Hulse
David Kingdom
Geoff Thomas

Soli Deo Gloria

...for instruction in righteousness...

Soli Deo Gloria Publications
213 W. Vincent Street, Ligonier, PA 15658-1139
(412) 238-7741/FAX (412) 238-3002

*

A Marvelous Ministry
*How the All-round Ministry of
C H Spurgeon Speaks to us Today*
is copyrighted 1993.

*

ISBN 1-877611-59-X

A Marvellous Ministry

How the All-round Ministry of C H Spurgeon Speaks to us Today

Foreword

'In the midst of the theologically discredited nineteenth century there was a preacher who had at least
six thousand people in his congregation every Sunday,
whose sermons for many years were cabled to New York
every Monday and reprinted in the leading newspapers
of the country, and who occupied the same pulpit for almost forty years without any diminishment in the flowing
abundance of his preaching and without ever repeating
himself or preaching himself dry. The fire he thus kin-
dled, and turned into a beacon that shone across the seas
and down through the generations was no mere brush
fire of sensationalism, but an inexhaustible blaze that
glowed and burned on solid hearths and was fed by the
wells of the eternal Word. Here was the miracle of a bush
that burned with fire and yet was not consumed.'

With these words Helmut Thielicke opened his classic study of
Charles Haddon Spurgeon, the greatest preacher to adorn the evangelical church since John Knox thundered in Scotland. During his
lifetime his voice was heard by an estimated 10 million persons; on
occasion he spoke to more than 20,000 persons at once and was heard
by all without the benefit of a public address system. Today, like
Abel, he being dead, yet speaks. Over against the flaccid sermons
and transcendence-starved theology of most contemporary preachers Spurgeon's writings continue to be republished, purchased and

read. In 1992, a century after his death, there were more works in print by Spurgeon than by any other English speaking author, living or dead.

However, Spurgeon was more than the prince of preachers. He was a mighty instrument of spiritual awakening, of revival and reformation, in an age when both the piety and theology of the church were under duress from without and within. The essays in this volume seek to move beyond the impression of Spurgeon as an affectionate celebrity. They deal instead with the real core of Spurgeon's true spiritual concerns. They show us what was so decisively at stake in the work he began, the ideas he set forth, the battles he waged.

Each of the authors is, like the subject, a convinced evangelical Baptist who stands firmly within the Reformed tradition. Together they bring a wealth of pastoral and scholarly experience to the labour of love. Their essays are like a mosaic touching in turn on four major themes in the marvellous ministry of Charles Haddon Spurgeon: his pastoral labours, his evangelistic outreach, his theological fidelity, and his social and political commitment.

Geoff Thomas presents an engaging portrait of Spurgeon's life from his boyhood days in Essex through his remarkable 37 years of ministry in London. Spurgeon's work at the Metropolitan Tabernacle has been compared to that of Whitefield at Moorgate. He was a superchurch pastor who knew every member of his congregation by name and who was never too busy to practise the holy art of dealing with anxious enquirers. He once said, 'If sinners will be damned, at least let them leap to hell over our bodies. And if they perish, let them perish with our arms about their knees, imploring them to stay. If hell must be filled, at least let it be filled in the teeth of our exertions, and let not one go there unwarned and unprayed for.'

Spurgeon was what the German Pietists called *ein Ganzer Christ*, 'A wholehearted Christian.' As he put it in his own quaint way, 'It seems to me if a man is a Christian, Christianity ought to eat him right up. It ought to go right through him.' His passion for souls, along with his extraordinary pulpit work, grew out of his close walk with God. The Bible was more than a resource book of sermons for him. His very blood was Bibline. He meditated daily on the Word of God and lived in a constant attitude of prayer. As Lewis Drummond has put it, 'He simply breathed the atmosphere of God's presence.'

Spurgeon cut his theological teeth on the writings of the great Puritan masters whose commitment to God's salvific sovereignty became the cornerstone of his own doctrinal system. He was unswervingly committed to the distinguishing doctrines of grace as set forth in the Second London Confession of 1689. Yet Spurgeon did not hesitate to oppose the kind of hyper-Calvinistic theology which, so he thought, had 'chilled many churches to their very soul,' leading them 'to omit the free invitations of the gospel, and to deny that it is the duty of sinners to believe in Jesus.' Erroll Hulse does a masterful job of showing how Spurgeon's evangelical Calvinism, far from being a hindrance, was itself the driving incentive in his universal preaching of the gospel. No one who reads this account of Spurgeon's gospel invitations should ever again be misled by the erroneous idea that Calvinism, balanced and biblical as Spurgeon's was, is antithetical either to the notion of human responsibility or to the evangelistic mandate of our Lord.

Nowhere is Spurgeon a more trustworthy or relevant guide for today's Church than in his courageous stand for historic Christianity in the Downgrade Controversy. David Kingdon places this dispute in proper historical context, outlines its main issues and makes several timely applications for the contemporary evangelical scene. Many of the doctrinal concerns which prompted Spurgeon's reaction are with us still: the character of the Holy Scripture as the infallible totally truthful Word of God; the finality of Jesus Christ as the only way of salvation for all peoples everywhere; the work of God of bringing into being the human race through a special act of creation; and the reality of eternal punishment over against theories of annihilation, second-chance salvation and universalism. Spurgeon sought to stave off the 'boiling mudshowers of modern heresy' which were beginning to descend on church life in his day by holding forth the standard of confessional Christianity. In our own era of compromise and con-cession, we need urgently to heed Spurgeon's appeal. The price of theological integrity, like that of liberty, is eternal vigilance.

No depiction of Spurgeon's all-round ministry would be com-plete without an examination of the social and political impact of his life's work. The essays by Tim Curnow and David Kingdon on these themes show us a Spurgeon whose compassion, charity and political engagement embody the best of 'the Nonconformist conscience' in nineteenth century England. It is instructive that one of the lead-ing defenders of theological orthodoxy was also one of the leading reformers and advocates of Christian social ministry and action.

A host of benevolent institutions grew up around Spurgeon's ministry: the Poor Ministers' Clothing Society; the Stockwell Or-phanage; The Pastor's School; the Book Fund Ministry; the Poor

Fund, a society organised to lend assistance to needy expectant mothers... all evidence that Spurgeon, like his Lord, 'went about doing good.' At the same time he never forgot (unlike many social gospellers of later times) that the fact of sin lay at the bottom of all the sorrow and social distresses in the world. For this reason he never ceased to repeat the message he had heard as a 15-year-old sinner at the Primitive Methodist Church in Colchester; 'Look to Jesus Christ! Look! Look! Look! You have nothing to do but look and live!'

The 'Last of the Puritans' has run his race and now waits, with all of the blessed departed, for the victory shout of Resurrection Morning. May the courage, commitment and vision of Charles Haddon Spurgeon inspire all of us who follow in his train to remain faithful to the ideals for which he expended his life, and in so doing remain faithful to Jesus Christ, his Lord and ours.

Timothy George
Dean, Beeson Divinity School
Samford University
Birmingham, Alabama, USA

About the contributors

Geoff Thomas, a graduate of Westminster Seminary, has for 27 years pastored the Alfred Place Baptist Church in Aberystwyth. He exercises a wide ministry not only in his home country of Wales but as a conference speaker in Britain and abroad. He is one of the editors of the monthly paper *Evangelical Times* and a regular and versatile contributor to that paper. Geoff is a brilliant biographer and has often opened the annual Carey Conference with a biography. This he did at the 1992 gathering when this chapter had its birth.

David Kingdon was principal of the Irish Baptist College before becoming pastor of the Lynnwood Baptist Church, Pretoria, South Africa. He is at present theological books editor with Inter Varsity Press which position affords him an outstanding perspective on contemporary Christian literature. He is pastorally active as an elder of Bethel Evangelical Free church, Wigston, Leicestershire. During the second world war he lost his father and was brought up for a number of years in Spurgeon's Orphanage. Thus in a very personal way he appreciates the social concern emanating from Spurgeon's ministry which he so ably expounds in these pages.

Tim Curnow is engaged in church planting work in Hemel Hempstead in Hertfordshire. His interest in William Gladstone led to a study of the subject of Spurgeon and his activity in politics. How can a minister be involved in politics when that can lead to many pitfalls and misunderstandings? This question is tackled with clarity in Tim Curnow's chapter.

Erroll Hulse has thirty years of pastoral experience and is at present associate pastor of the Leeds Reformed Baptist Church. He is a member of the executive committee of the International Fellowship of Reformed Baptists and the editor of its international bi-monthly journal *Reformation Today* and the author of several books the most recent of which are *'The Great Invitation'* and *'Give Him no Rest'*, both published by Evangelical Press.

Preface

During the centenary year of Spurgeon's death in 1892, meetings were held in various parts of Britain. Interest in the relevance of Spurgeon's life and ministry has reawakened, bringing with it the bonus of materials, some of which have been selected and especially prepared for this book.

It is always refreshing to read of the way in which one so young was thrust into the pastorate at Waterbeach, and then at New Park Street in London. The romance and excitement of that is relived in the biography of Geoff Thomas, who has dug out a number of fascinating features which are not found in the popular biographies. The other chapters are devoted to important doctrinal and practical issues which tend to be overlooked.

The first chapter, *Spurgeon Speaks Today*, is designed as a general introduction to the book.

Chapters 2, 3, and 4 originated at the Carey Minister's Conference in January 1992. Two of the papers appeared in *Reformation Today* number 126, but the first two sections of chapter 3 have been extended. Chapter 5 was originally presented at the Puritan (now Westminster) Conference at Westminster Chapel, London, in 1971.

Chapter 6 was prepared for this book by Tim Curnow. Interest in Spurgeon, and his involvement in politics, has increased following the research by Dr. Patricia Kruppa, whose thesis on Spurgeon has not been published, but can be obtained through public libraries.

The book has been edited by Erroll Hulse and David Kingdon. The four editors are indebted to Eward North of Harrogate for his generosity in collating all the parts on disk, and to Don Kistler of Soli Deo Gloria Ministries for his versatile role as publisher.

Chapters

Contents

Chapter 1

Spurgeon Speaks Today

Charles Haddon Spurgeon passed to his eternal reward in 1892 yet his life and ministry continue to speak to us in a most relevant way today.

By way of introducing this book I would like to outline ten ways in which Spurgeon speaks to us today. The first six points stem mostly from his life which is described by Geoff Thomas while points seven to ten are derived from other chapters of the book, and will serve to introduce those themes. That there are ten points is accidental, which also happens to be the case with the chapter on Spurgeon and his gospel invitations.

The great Baptist preacher was not perfect. Exceedingly gifted leaders can be imperious and Spurgeon often gave that impression. I mention this lest readers get the impression that we are adulating a leader. Throughout we need to observe the glory of Christ in taking a frail body as the apostle Paul declares, 'But we have this treasure in jars of clay to show that this all-surpassing power is from God and not from us' (2 Cor 4:7). Ephesians 4:11 says that our ascended Lord gave some to be pastors. He gives gifts to his church. He prepares and trains them. He uses them and upholds them. From the outset then let us give the glory to the Head of the Church.

1.1   Spurgeon's life speaks to us today as an example of the advantages of a godly upbringing

Spurgeon's parents were godly and much appreciated as his letters to them reveal.[1] But by far the most significant influence on Charles as a child was his grandfather. CHS records 'When I was a very little child, I lived so long with my grandfather that he became everything to me.'[2] Geoff Thomas explains the circumstances which brought about the advantageous position whereby the child prodigy was to enjoy the additional benefit of the constant and affectionate attention of his grandparents at Stambourne together with an aunt who was still at home. Grandfather James was a wonderful preacher who drew a large congregation to Stambourne village. Many would walk long distances to hear him. Later when Charles had become famous he noticed occasional visitors in his London congregation from the Stambourne area and he asked them what brought them such a distance. Their response was most revealing, "We would run our legs off to hear a Spurgeon", was the reply. In other words they were looking for a preacher with the same spiritual unction as the Spurgeon of Stambourne. The child was the subject not only of his family's tuition but also of their prayers. For every Isaac Watts hymn learned by heart he received a reward. His knowledge not only of Watts but of hymns generally was seen in his ability to instantly recall appropriate verses while preaching and is to observed in his published sermons.

Geoff Thomas also describes the unusual providence of the provision of the valuable Puritan Henry Havers library which was bequeathed to the Stambourne rectory and thereby made accessible to young Charles. It is one thing for books to be available and another to have the desire to read them. It is usually the enthusiastic recommendation of others that activates our own interest in books and it is difficult to imagine the boy would take an interest in such ponderous volumes were it not for his grandfather's zest for the gospel.

A godly upbringing does not preclude fun. All his life Charles enjoyed an acute sense of humour which was also a feature of his Grandad. On one occasion when James was asked how much he weighed, he answered, "Well that all depends on how you take me.

---

[1] *The Early Years*, chapter 9
[2] *Metropolitan Tabernacle Pulpit*, 1909, p 604

If weighed in the balances I am afraid I shall be found wanting, but in the pulpit they tell me I am heavy enough!"

The home is the workshop where the future generation is trained. Let us never underestimate the importance of constant quality time and attention given to our children.

1.2 Spurgeon speaks to us today by reminding us of the importance of a godly marriage.

The biblical institution of marriage is under attack today. The first requirement for office in the church, whether for the diaconate or for the eldership, is a stable, well-run household. If a man cannot run his household well how can he take charge of the affairs of the church?

Arnold Dallimore in his popular biography of Spurgeon published by the Banner of Truth for his chapter *Spurgeon's Marriage*, has a subtitle: 'This one truly made in heaven'. Yet this suggestion too easily gives a wrong impression that Mr and Mrs Spurgeon had an ideal marriage in every respect which is certainly not the case. Mrs Spurgeon was an invalid most of her life and experienced much pain and isolation. What should be noted is that grace was given and patience and love exercised under such circumstances. There were spiritual resources upon which to draw to meet the difficulties. Today the unrealistic and harmful Hollywood concept prevails, that is, that everything in marriage should be fun and sunshine. Unity in a Christian marriage can be strengthened in sharing together the setbacks and the problems and overcoming the incompatibilities which may not have been foreseen.

In spite of her handicap Mrs Spurgeon developed a prolific work of supplying books to pastors. Such was her devotion that she built up a list of 6,000 names (mostly ministers and students) who received books through the book fund which she established. She organised a team of helpers for that work and kept a record of every title dispatched.

The gift of partnership is a priceless gift to be cherished and nurtured. Spurgeon's marriage is an example of a Christian partnership working in spite of severe problems.

1.3   Spurgeon speaks to us to today as an example of consistent Church Membership.

Although his parents and grandparents were Congregationalists and not Baptists, young Charles at his conversion, aged 15, had thought through the issues concerning baptism and church membership. He early grasped the importance of being integrated into church membership and perceived at the same time the importance of the biblical order that baptism should precede participation at the Lord's Table. Although invited he declined coming to the Lord's table until he had been baptised.

For him church membership was a living responsibility and he sought from the outset to serve within the body of the local church. Later when he became the leader of a huge congregation he sought that every member had some role and some work to do. This emerges clearly in the chapter by David Kingdon 'Spurgeon and his Social Concern.' The preacher at the Metropolitan Tabernacle was not looking for pew warmers or spectators but expected that every member be active.

1.4   Spurgeon speaks to us today by showing us that the stated means of grace are adequate

Over the last decade or two there has been a strong movement within the believing Church of Christ, to go in search of prophecies, miracles and supernatural gifts. Until recently it has been accepted by the Church as a whole that miracle working was the special province of Christ and his apostles. Because the achievement of Christ in our redemption is complete the testimony which establishes that is now sealed by the Scriptures. Therefore we do not stand in need of further proofs or evidences.

Those who believe in the continuation of apostolic miracles would largely agree with the above but they argue plausibly that miracles not only act as a proof of the genuine nature of the gospel but serve to arrest the attention of the unbelieving secular-minded public. We are left wondering if our cause is an utterly forlorn one. How can the gospel succeed if it is to depend on preaching alone?

Spurgeon arrived in a city which was as unspiritual as London is today. It is true that church attendance was more in vogue, but the fact is that Spurgeon's ministry was a converting ministry unassisted by signs and wonders. Spurgeon refused even the assistance of an organ. It was the preaching that God blessed. There were baptisms and there was the Lord's Table as well as all kinds of outreach, but nothing which went in any way beyond the plain means of grace. This should encourage us greatly today. The plain means of grace, prayer, teaching and preaching require constant effort. These keep us dependent and humble. They have been the mark of every revival and spiritual awakening since the apostolic age. The spiritual awakening under Spurgeon was no exception. In that way he speaks to us today.

1.5   Spurgeon's life reminds us of the necessity of a specific call to the ministry

In 1875 *'Lectures to my Students'* was published. Its relevance is as timely now as it was then. The second chapter is devoted to the call to the ministry. This was something about which the great preacher felt passionately.

He begins the chapter on *The Call to the Ministry* by defining the office of both teaching and bearing rule in the church as one 'which requires the dedication of a man's entire life to spiritual work, and separation from every secular calling' (2 Tim 2:4). 'If any student in this room could be content to be a newspaper editor, or a grocer, or a farmer, or a doctor, or a lawyer, or a senator, or a king, in the name of heaven and earth let him go his way.'

Spurgeon contended with the Plymouth Brethren about this matter: 'The Plymouthist strives to get rid of the pastorate, but he never can, for the Lord will ever continue to give pastors after his own heart to feed his people, and all attempts made by the flock to dispose of these pastors will lead to leanness and poverty of soul.'[3]

This view of a call to the ministry corrects the idea prevalent in some quarters that all elders are equal. There is parity or equality when in session to lead the affairs of the church, but not equality in terms of calling and gifts. Those who leave their secular callings are

---

[3] *Metropolitan Tabernacle Pulpit,* 1862, p 195 cited in *Reformation Today* 114

vulnerable. Their vocation is different and always has been. Spurgeon saw that clearly and so we need to today.

1.6   Spurgeon is an example to us with regard to financial integrity

In recent years we have been saddened by the bad example of some tele-evangelists who have accrued fortunes and adopted worldly and extravagant lifestyles far removed from the example of Christ.

Spurgeon had some extravagant attitudes but throughout his life he was generous to others and when he died he left behind relatively very little by way of accrued wealth.

During the first years of the college he bore the entire financial responsibility for the students, depending largely on the income from his books and sermons. In the maintenance of the almshouses when money was not donated for several years he paid for the heat, light and other expenses from his own pocket. Later when the Tabernacle gave him a generous gift to commemorate his quarter century of ministry he gave it all away to his charitable concerns, the almshouses receiving half of it. He frequently gave away the money given to him for preaching engagements. His disinterest in lucre and his generosity to others reminds us of our personal responsibility to be generous and cheerful givers.

1.7   Spurgeon speaks today through his consistently clear evangelistic preaching

From first to last Spurgeon was an evangelist. For him every service represented an evangelistic opportunity. The fact that Spurgeon's coming to London in 1854 was a harbinger of the 1858-9 spiritual awakening has mostly been overlooked. Certainly to the best of my knowledge that particular issue has not been the subject of concentrated research. For this reason in the chapter on the character of Spurgeon's Gospel invitations I described the historical background which enables the reader to appreciate the fact that while Spurgeon expounded the Word of God in an exemplary way he did not follow the systematic consecutive method.

The appeal is sometimes made for a simple gospel which too often means a superficial gospel. The strength and depth of the gospel preached by Spurgeon was that it was integral with solid doctrinal foundations. Many struggle to reconcile the absolute sovereign purpose of God in salvation with the total responsibility of man to believe and repent. Again referring to the chapter on his Gospel invitations the clear and decisive nature of Spurgeon's Calvinism is explained since that was the bed-rock from which his gospel appeals were made. There was a marvellous aptitude, variety and compulsion about those gospel appeals, from which we can be inspired and instructed today.

1.8 Spurgeon speaks to us today with regard to works of compassion

That Jesus cared about the poor and needy was transparently evident in his ministry. He was constantly attending to the sick and handicapped. How do we know that he cares today? We know by the work of compassion provided by his disciples.

Anyone visiting the Metropolitan Tabernacle during the last century would be left in no doubt about the message of salvation and the way of justification by faith, but the church's many ministries of compassion would leave that person in no doubt that Christ now cares through his people. David Kingdon defines the roots of Spurgeon's social concern. He describes the various ways in which social concern was put into practice. This theme is highly relevant for us today.

1.9 Spurgeon speaks to us today as an example of effective influence on politicians

Tim Curnow explains how Spurgeon influenced politicians and draws out principles aimed to help us understand how this can be done. This is important because there are many who oppose any involvement by Christians in politics. But politics like religion is a subject with enormous breadth and ramifications. Politics embraces both civil government and civil law. It is simply not possible to ignore politics when those politics infringe on morals and the way we live. We can hardly afford political hibernation in contemporary society when

we see that society drifting more and more into anti-Christian philosophy and lawlessness. For example, in the United States of America
the battle for a moral base in schools is all but lost. Many have given
up the contest and opted for Christian schools as the only way forward. That option is not viable in most countries.

Another issue which is coming to the fore is that of the rights of
parents. Recently the Law Commission in Scotland proposed legis-
lation forbidding parents to smack their children. Some hailed this
as a triumph for childrens' rights. This subject is becoming a contro-
versial issue which is being contested in the courts in Britain. There
are many other moral issues about which the church cannot be silent;
issues which require to be addressed by Christian statesmen.

The powerful way in which Spurgeon influenced the politics of
his day is an example for us. Therein he still speaks.

1.10   Spurgeon speaks to us today about faith- fulness in contending for the truth

The Downgrade in the Baptist Union from which Spurgeon resigned
in 1887 is typical of other downward movements from fidelity to in-
fidelity. There has been a Downgrade in the huge Southern Baptist
denomination of the USA. The battle in the Southern Baptist Con-
vention continues today and it is by no means lost. A Downgrade
into Liberalism has occurred in the Free University of Amsterdam
which was previously a bastion for the Reformed Faith. A Downgrade has been taking place in the major Dutch Reformed Church
of South Africa (NG Kerk).

The issues that confronted Spurgeon are the same as face those
in Downgrade situations today. Three matters demand a biblical response. First there was the issue of false teachers. What is the Scriptural response to liberal clergymen whose teachings overthrow the
gospel? Second, what is the correct biblical response to evangelical
ministers who compromise with and cooperate with false teachers?
Third, in contending for the truth where do we draw the line: do
we contend for a full confessional basis or do we cling only to truth
essential to salvation?

Firstly, Spurgeon saw clearly that Modernism was antithetical to
the gospel. He would have nothing to do with liberal teachers, which
position is in accord with the guidance of Galatians 1:8 and 2 John

9,10. He opposed Modernism in a biblical manner.

Spurgeon has been criticised for not answering the claims of the Liberals in the same thorough way as B B Warfield whose writings not only refuted higher critical claims but strengthened many in their faith. This criticism of Spurgeon overlooks the fact that he was primarily an evangelist-pastor and not a polemicist or apologist. He was famous for his preaching not for learned treatises. His great seven volume commentary on the Psalms was the result of team work. Spurgeon must be given credit for seeing clearly that modernism is unbelief dressed up in the fine clothes of scholarship and that it is a system with which there can be no compromise. The advance of Modernism in the Baptist Union compelled his resignation from that body.

Secondly, he sought to maintain personal contact and sustain a personal relationship with evangelical ministers who compromised and were too weak to uphold the biblical position as outlined above. He reasoned with them. He was patient with them. He broke fellowship with them as far as cooperation was concerned, but he did not sever lines of personal communication with fellow ministers who compromised. He was sorrowful and reluctant in separating from brother ministers who refused to make a stand. Herein Spurgeon speaks to us today. Wherever possible we need to keep lines of communication open. But we cannot in good conscience join evangelicals on a public platform if that platform is occupied at the same time by those who are known liberals who themselves deny the gospel.

We must never cease in our personal efforts to persuade fellow evangelical ministers to desist from public cooperation with liberals and it is important too to discourage the support of liberal seminaries which undermine and destroy the faith of students.

Thirdly, he set an example with regard to clear thinking as to where we draw the line with regard to truth. From the outset, Spurgeon built upon the doctrinal foundation of the 1689 London Baptist Confession of Faith. Throughout his ministry he uncompromisingly preached the distinctives of that Reformed Confession. He expected those of a different church order such as Presbyterians to proclaim their confessional standards. It was precisely because he was so clear and powerful as a gospel preacher that all the doctrines organically connected to that gospel could be proclaimed and subsumed in their right order and proportion.

He regarded evangelical unity as paramount. When many were unfaithful to the gospel he did not sever fraternal relationships or

regard cooperation with other ministers as futile. In the early months
of 1890 he joined together with six others in a fraternal with a basis
of faith which was evangelical, Calvinistic and pre-millennial.[4] This
fraternal was not confined to Baptists and soon grew to about thirty
pastors.

Spurgeon was willing to cohere with other evangelicals on the basis of primary truth, that is truth essential for salvation. But we can
sense that he was uneasy about the idea that some truths can be regarded as secondary lest that might undermine the gospel. As we
have noted, theology is organic. Its doctrines are interrelated. The
stance taken on one truth affects the construction of others. The
battle is always changing. What was regarded as a secondary truth
yesterday may become primary today. Luther pointed out we need
to defend the Faith specifically where it is under attack. That attack
varies constantly. New dangers threaten the Church. Increasingly
ours is a pluralistic society and the pressure is mounting on evangelicals to compromise the uniqueness of the gospel as the only way
of salvation. We are required to think issues through for ourselves.
Spurgeon's example can inspire us to be courageous and faithful. He
was never reckless but he was firm and resolute, despite experiencing
rejection and deep discouragement. We need to hold the truth and
contend for it in a loving manner as he did.

Spurgeon speaks to us today because he was so powerful as a
gospel preacher and under the gospel was able to subsume and
comprehend so many other important issues without getting side-
tracked. It was because he was so eminent as a gospel preacher that
63 volumes of his sermons continue to be used today.

In many ways we have seen an upgrade during the last two or
three decades, the upgrade which Spurgeon declared would come,
(see David Kingdon's chapter on the Downgrade). Even though we
have seen a turning of the tide in what may be called a theological
renewal we have not even remotely experienced anything of the spiritual awakening which was so marked in Spurgeon's ministry. We
long and pray for revival but whatever the immediate future holds,
we are grateful for what has been handed down to us by that prince
of preachers, and we are grateful for the way in which his life and
ministry speaks to us today.

When he died, as Geoff Thomas shows at the conclusion of his
biography, there were those who were hostile to him personally and

---

[4] *Sword and Trowel*, August 1891 pp 389–90

exceedingly resentful and disparaging about his stand for the truth. Yet today they are forgotten but he continues to speak to us. May that be so yet further to Christ's glory.

Chapter 2

The Preacher's Progress

Charles Haddon Spurgeon was born in Kelvedon, Essex in June 1834, and died far away from that centre of English protestantism in the south of France in Hotel Beau Rivage (which has recently been demolished) at the beautiful Riviera town of Mentone, near the Italian border, on January 31st 1892.

Essex is the county nearest the continent of Europe which, in the 16th century, had borne the brunt of anti-protestant persecution during Queen Mary's reign. The greatest density of martyrs from any part of the British Isles was found there. Under the succeeding reign of Elizabeth it welcomed protestant exiles from the continent, so that throughout the next hundred years Puritanism flourished in the east of England as nowhere else. The Act of Uniformity of 1662 commanded universal adoption of the Elizabethan Prayer Book. All ministers had publicly to give their 'unfeigned consent and assent' to the Book and obtain episcopal ordination if not so ordained. A declaration of loyalty and repudiation of the National Covenant had also to be taken. These provisions led to the 'Great Ejection' of about 2,000 evangelical preachers, the final parting of the ways between Anglicans and Puritans and the consequent birth of English Nonconformity.

Many Christian families in Essex followed their preachers out of the Church of England into non-conformity. A certain Job Spurgeon spent 15 months in Chelmsford jail for attending a non-conformist meeting. Essex was again the county with the largest population of Protestant nonconformists in the 1676 census. In one community, a village called Stambourne, they were actually in the majority. The

13

rector had been Henry Havers, a Cambridge graduate, whose congregation followed him out of the church in 1662. The Toleration Act
of William and Mary in 1689 resulted in a large Independent Meeting
House being erected in the centre of the village. Havers purchased
the plot of land on which the manse and chapel were built. He supervised the erection of that chapel with its galleries on three sides
which could hold, in all, about 200 people. Havers willed the manse
and his substantial library of Puritan works to his successors in the
Stambourne pastorate.

Several lengthy ministries preceded the advent of James Spurgeon to the pastorate at Stambourne. James, born in 1776, was himself to have a long ministry of 58 years at Stambourne from 1810.
He inherited the library of Henry Havers. The Stambourne congregation had only four ministers in the course of two hundred years.
James had ten children, the second of whom was his son John who became a book keeper to a coal merchant, but on Sundays he preached
in a small Independent church in Tollesbury. He became the father
of 17 children, 8 of whom survived infancy. Charles Haddon Spurgeon was the first-born child, and his two youngest sisters, Josephine
and Flora, were in fact born after the birth of his own twin sons when
he was the pastor of the New Park Street church in London. At this
time his father had become minister in a church in Islington in north
London.

Before his first birthday Charles was sent to Stambourne to live
with his grandparents and their 15-year old daughter, Ann, spending
the first five years of his life there, but often returning to that manse
subsequently for lengthy visits. He became his grandparents' delight.
The village of Stambourne had a population of 500 people inhabiting
100 cottages. His grandfather rarely left that community, never visiting London. Stambourne had remained virtually unchanged from
the time of Henry Havers, and Spurgeon idealised the community.
In the last months of his life in 1891 he returned back to this village
of his childhood. By then he had preached his last sermon: his body
was racked with kidney failure. He went to view again the peace of
the village scene and recapture the happiness of his infant memories.
He was writing his last book *Memories of Stambourne* and in it he
tells his readers that all had changed. The old chapel and manse had
been demolished. The green pastures were swampy after rain. The
country lanes were knee deep in mud. A chill wind came blowing
through the woods. His grandfather's country was no more. There
can be no return to paradise while men are in this world.

2.1   Childhood

The child Charles Haddon Spurgeon was soon to discover that his grandfather James was an imposing figure in the area. The vicar, James Hopkins, was a brother in the faith preaching the same gospel, and every Monday afternoon the two Jameses, accompanied by the little boy, went for tea at the home of the village squire and discussed the problems and spiritual state of the community. Charles was a bright child with a superior memory. His schoolmates said that he 'led the class' and without making any effort he acquired knowledge. He was soon reading and immediately was into the Bible, Bunyan, Fox and Havers' library of Puritans. They were all to be found off an upstairs bedroom in a little study which was in total darkness (the windows having been blocked to avoid paying the window-duty); the lack of light could have assisted in their preservation. From there Spurgeon would drag into daylight some enormous folios, too heavy for him to lift — 'the great masters of Scriptural theology, with whom no moderns are worthy to be named in the same day,' he was to say. No preacher in the last 300 years became more familiar with Puritan writers; he was able to make a considered judgment on the worth of thousands of books and absorb their convictions translating them into the most contemporary awakening ministry.

The conversation in the manse was full of the Bible and pastoral concerns. The boy became somewhat precocious; his Aunt Ann, who out-lived him by almost ten years, remembers when the four of them were talking about the inconsistent behaviour of one of the church members called Tom Roads. Charles was upset at this man causing his grandfather such distress: "I'll kill him!" he cried. His grandfather calmed his concerns, and expressed his disapproval of any harm being done to the prodigal. Yet he was perplexed the next day when the boy returned home with the message, "I've killed old Roads and he will never grieve Grandpa anymore." Within a few hours Tom Roads himself appeared sheepishly at the manse to reveal how he had been drinking at the village public house when the boy had come marching up to him and looked him in the eye saying: "What doest thou here Elijah? Sitting with the ungodly, and you a member of the church, and breaking your pastor's heart. I'm ashamed of you! I wouldn't break my pastor's heart." Tom Roads's initial anger turned to conviction and he came to apologise to James Spurgeon, and to reform his ways. (James Spurgeon was succeeded at Stambourne by John Houchin and he pastored Tom Roads in the last four years of his life. He was a simple man whose livelihood was a pony and cart. He never learned to read, and during the final weeks of his life he laboriously counted all the pages of his Bible: "I never could read a word of it, but thought I would know how many pages it had.")

While his grandmother gave the boy a penny for every Isaac Watts hymn he learned by heart his grandfather gave the young Spurgeon a shilling for every rat he killed! After his first long period in the Stambourne manse he had to return to live with his parents, and both he and his grandfather were upset at the parting: "Now child, tonight, when the moon shines and you look at it, don't forget that it is the same moon your grandfather will be looking at."

The influence of Charles's own parents' was also considerable. His affection for his father was legendary: he once said, "I know that the words of my father with me alone, when he prayed with me, and bade me pray for myself — not to use any form of prayer, but to pray just as I felt, and to ask from God what I felt that I really wanted — left an impression upon my mind that will never be erased." His mother would always lead the family devotions when his father was away preaching. Charles could reminisce, "I heard my mother say as she sat talking to us children about our souls, that she did not believe there was a single living man who dared to declare that he truly sought the Saviour and that the Saviour had refused him. She said she did not think that even in hell there was one who would be bold enough to accuse the Saviour of having refused him when he sought him with prayer and in faith." Elizabeth Spurgeon would read to the children Alleine's *Alarm to the Unconverted.* "O that book !" said Spurgeon. "How many dreams it gave her boy at night about the devouring flames and the everlasting burnings."

Outside the family circle there were other influences molding the values of the boy. There was a farmer called Will Richardson who was very patient and wise with the boy. Charles would scamper off to the farm to accompany the farmer at his chores, and Mr. Richardson was full of shrewd observations and common sense, especially in applying the Scripture in a natural way. He was to become the model for a character Spurgeon created called '*John Ploughman*.' His books of observations about such subjects as 'The Preacher's Appearance', 'Men with Two Faces', 'A hand-saw is a good thing, but not to shave with' and 'Great cry and little wool, as the man said who clipped the sow', sold hundreds of thousands of copies.

Another person Spurgeon met when he was a teenager was the cook-cum-matron at his school, a woman named Mary King. She subscribed to the *Gospel Standard* magazine and was able to talk to him about the doctrines of grace. One or two of those conversations were especially significant in settling in his mind an understanding of the sovereignty of God in redemption.

Charles Haddon Spurgeon never lost his desire to listen to those who were not clergymen and to profit from their observations. He related his perplexity at one period concerning the problem of why God should hear the prayers of an unconverted child. He describes the woman who helped him as 'wearing a red cloak', and that she had replied simply that if God hears the cry of young ravens then he surely hears the prayers of his higher creatures, though unsaved. The comment was simple, but Spurgeon clung to it. As he was to say in an early sermon in his first year at the New Park Street Pulpit, "For my own part I desire to be somewhat a student of the heart, and I think I have learned far more from conversation with my fellow men than I ever did from reading." Spurgeon was in good company: two walked to Emmaus with One who conversed and opened up Scripture to them and made their hearts burn within them. John Bunyan 'came where there were three or four poor women sitting at a door in the sun, and talking about the things of God' and his own heart began to shake. Lord Shaftesbury became a Christian through the influence of Maria Millis, the maid to his mother.

It was at a school in Newmarket where Charles was a sort of junior assistant teacher (known as an 'usher') that a fellow usher kept a diary and recorded that his 15 year-old friend was 'a clever pleasant little fellow ... small and delicate, with a pale but plump face, dark brown eyes and hair, and a bright lively manner, with a never failing flow of conversation.' He was uninterested in games, poor in co-ordination and clumsy, fearful of crowds of people or of a herd of cows on the road. At maturity his height was 5 feet 6 inches. He occasionally tried to ride a horse but confessed, "I feel such intense love for Mother Earth that before long I embrace her." He described his ideal horse as "quiet, safe, old and blind." Spurgeon lived in the age of the railway train.

2.2   Conversion

There is a chapter in his autobiography entitled, *Through Much Tribulation* and page after page describes the intense spiritual struggle Spurgeon experienced before coming into an assurance that he

was a true Christian. The story is one of the most moving and carefully documented records of conversion in the history of the church.
Spurgeon had heard preachers say how easy it was to become a Christian: "I really thought that I could turn to Christ when I pleased, and
that therefore I could put it off to the last part of my life, when it
might be conveniently done upon a sick-bed. But when the Lord
gave my soul its first shakings in conviction, I soon knew better."
Spurgeon was reading Bunyan's *Grace Abounding*, Baxter's *Call* and
John Angell James's *The Anxious Inquirer*, all of which sustained his
conviction of his need of God's grace. He was to describe this period
as being 'in the custody of the law'. He spoke of it soberly:

> 'I recollect that experience, and how I thought of
> what was said of the old Roman empire that, under the
> rule of Cæsar, if a man once broke the law of Rome,
> he was in prison everywhere. The whole world was one
> vast prison to him, for he could not get out of the reach
> of the imperial power; and so did it come to be in my
> aroused conscience. Wherever I went, the law had a de-
> mand upon my thoughts, upon my words, upon my rising,
> upon my resting. What I did, and what I did not do, all
> came under the cognizance of the law; and then I found
> that this law so surrounded me that I was always running
> against it, I was always breaking it. I seemed as if I was
> a sinner, and nothing else but a sinner. If I opened my
> mouth I spoke amiss. If I sat still, there was sin in my si-
> lence. I remember that, when the Spirit of God was thus
> dealing with me, I used to feel myself to be a sinner even
> when I was in the house of God. I thought that, when I
> sang, I was mocking the Lord with a solemn sound upon
> a false tongue; and if I prayed, I feared that I was sin-
> ning in my prayers, insulting him by uttering confessions
> which I did not feel, and asking for mercies with a faith
> that was not true at all, but only another form of unbe-
> lief. Oh yes, some of us know what it is to be given into
> custody to the law!
>
> 'Then the law, as interpreted by Christ, said, "Whoso-
> ever looketh on a woman to lust after her hath commit-
> ted adultery with her already in his heart." The law said,
> "Thou shalt not steal," and I said, "Well, I never stole
> anything;" but then I found that even the desire to pos-

sess what was not my own was guilt. Then the law informed me that I was cursed unless I continued in all things that were written in the book of the law to do them. So I saw that I was "shut up".'[1]

2.3   Free at Last

The experience by which Spurgeon was delivered from that burden of the condemning law is the best known conversion in the history of the Church. The event is referred to on 26 occasions in the 63 volumes of his sermons. But that reiteration is dwarfed by references to his time of humbling under the conviction of sin which are found on no less than 58 occasions.

It was on a wintry Sunday, January 6 1850, his school being temporarily closed because of an outbreak of fever, that the 15 year-old Spurgeon found himself in Colchester and on his way to his Congregational Chapel. The snow and sleet intensified so that he turned down a side lane called Artillery Street and came across a Primitive Methodist Church. It is any port in a storm, and so the teenager entered this building for the first time to attend the morning service. There were no more than fifteen people present: even the minister had failed to arrive because of the weather. It was the wrong church, the wrong congregation, the wrong weather and the wrong preacher. Into the pulpit climbed a thin-looking man, a shoemaker or tailor, Spurgeon was never to know anything about him. He announced his text as Isaiah 45:22, 'Look unto me, and be ye saved, all the ends of the earth: for I am God and there is none else.' Spurgeon remembered him saying in his broad Essex accent, 'Many on ye are lookin' to yourselves. But it's no use lookin' there. You'll never find any comfort in yourselves. Some say look to God, the Father. No, look to Him by-and-by. Jesus Christ says, "Look unto Me." Some on ye say, "We must wait for the Spirit's workin'". You have no business with that just now. Look to Christ. The text says, "Look unto Me".'

The preacher managed to spin that out for ten minutes and then, running out of anything fresh to say, looked at his congregation and picked on Spurgeon. "Young man, you look very miserable," he said, "and you always will be miserable — miserable in life and miserable in death — if you don't obey my text; but if you obey now, this mo-

---

[1] *Metropolitan Tabernacle Pulpit*, 1895, p 101ff

ment, you will be saved." And then he shouted at the top of his voice, "Young man, look to Jesus Christ. Look! Look! Look! You have nothing to do but to look and live!" Spurgeon later said, 'I thank God that I owe my conversion to Christ to an unknown person, who certainly was no minister in the ordinary acceptation of the term; but who could say this much, "Look unto Christ and be saved, all ye ends of the earth".'[2] Both his sons were to be converted through preachers whom they did not know.

Spurgeon said that that was the moment when he first grasped experientially one crucial truth, 'that salvation was in and through another, that my salvation could not be of myself, but must be through one better and stronger than I. And I heard — and oh, what music it was — that the Son of God had taken upon himself our human nature, and had, by his life and death, wrought out a perfect salvation, finished from top to bottom, which he was ready to give to every soul that was willing to have it, and that salvation was of grace from first to last, the free gift of God through his blessed Son, Jesus Christ ... That law-work, of which I have told you, had hammered me into such a condition that, if there had been fifty other saviours, I could not have thought of them, I was driven to this One.'[3]

When the congregation sang a hallelujah before they went out into the snow Spurgeon could join with them and as he walked back home the words of David kept ringing through his heart, 'Wash me and I shall be whiter than snow.' God flooded his heart with joy and assurance. Spurgeon described it like this: 'I looked to Jesus, and he looked on me; and we were one for ever. That moment my joy surpassed all bounds, just as my sorrow had aforetime driven me to an extreme of grief. I was perfectly at rest in Christ, satisfied with him, and my heart was glad; but I did not know that this grace was everlasting life till I began to read in the Scriptures, and to know more fully the value of the jewel which God had given me.'[4]

The change was immediately observed by his family: 'I remember standing before the fire, leaning on the mantelshelf, after I got home, and my mother spoke to me, and I heard her say outside the door, "There is a change come over Charles." She had not had half-a-dozen words with me; but she saw that I was not what I had been. I had been dull, melancholic, sorrowful, depressed; and when I had

[2] *Metropolitan Tabernacle Pulpit*, 1893, p 512
[3] *Metropolitan Tabernacle Pulpit*, 1895, p 101ff
[4] *Metropolitan Tabernacle Pulpit*, 1885, p 395

looked to Christ, the appearance of my face changed; I had a smile, a cheerful, happy, contented look at once, and she could see it; and a few words let her know that her melancholic boy had risen out of his despondency, and had become bright and cheerful.'[5] Until her death 38 years later she was to see that happy transformation sustained in her first-born child. That night he waited for the other children to go to bed before confiding with his father what had happened. By the middle of February he was calling once a week with a tract at 33 homes.

2.4 The Return To Artillery Street

The following Sunday Spurgeon returned to the Primitive Methodist Church in Artillery Street. He said, 'The next Sunday I went to the same chapel, as it was very natural that I should. But I never went back afterwards, for this reason, that during my first week the new life that was in me had been compelled to fight for its existence, and a conflict with the old nature had been vigorously carried on. This I knew to be a special token of the indwelling of grace in my soul. But in that same chapel I heard a sermon upon Romans 7:24, 'O wretched man that I am! who shall deliver me from the body of this death?' And the preacher declared that Paul was not a Christian when he had that experience. Babe as I was, I knew better than to believe so absurd a statement. I resolved to go into that pasture no more, for I could not feed therein.'[6]

Spurgeon's next visit to that church was 14 years later to preach at its anniversary services to 500 people packed into every corner. He chose as his text Isaiah 45:22 and pointed out the place he had occupied that January morning in 1850. There is still a gospel witness in Artillery Street in Colchester. Today it is called 'The Spurgeon Memorial Evangelical Church' and on November 30, 1991 Derek Hale was inducted as the pastor. The present membership consists of 4 people.

---

[5] *Metropolitan Tabernacle Pulpit*, 1892, p 464
[6] *Metropolitan Tabernacle Pulpit*, 1885, p 395

2.5 Baptism

Spurgeon had been attending a Church of England school during the previous year and it was during this time that he rejected infant baptism. He became acquainted with the Anglican catechism, and especially its answer to the question, 'What is required of persons to be baptised?' The answer was, 'Repentance, whereby they forsake sin; and faith, whereby they steadfastly believe the promises of God made to them in that sacrament.' Spurgeon checked that answer in the Bible: 'I found it strictly correct as far as repentance and faith are concerned; and, of course, when I afterwards became a Christian, I also became a Baptist; and here I am, and it is due to the Church of England catechism that I am a Baptist.'[7]

That is a typical piece of Spurgeonic roguery. Other reasons for his decision were an independent frame of mind, the influence of the Baptist headmaster at his new school in Newmarket (though at the time of his baptism he had not heard of the existence of Baptists),[8] his own study of the New Testament, and his longings, after so profound and thorough a conversion experience, for the public congregational demonstration of his new life in Christ. 'Parents, friends, all differed, but believer's baptism seemed to me to be scriptural, and, though I was a lad, God gave me grace to be honest to my conscience, and to follow the Lord in that respect as fully as I could.'[9] Even then he did not take the step inadvisedly: he said, 'My parents, not believing in the baptism of believers, and I, being between fifteen and sixteen years of age, thought it my duty to consult my father and mother, and ask their counsel and advice. I think I did right; I did not expect them to see with me, but I did expect them to give me their loving concurrence, which they did.'[10]

It was in the river Lark upon his mother's birthday, Friday, May 3rd, four months after his Artillery Street conversion, that he was immersed. He rose early that morning, spent two quiet hours alone with God in prayer, walked eight miles along the country lanes thinking of his indebtedness to his Saviour and his desire to live to his glory, and arrived at the river where a crowd of people were gathered. He said, 'I always feel glad that I wore a boy's jacket when I was baptised into his name; I had not assumed the garb of a man, but my whole soul

[7] *Metropolitan Tabernacle Pulpit*, 1893, p 354
[8] *Metropolitan Tabernacle Pulpit*, 1880, p 90
[9] *Metropolitan Tabernacle Pulpit*, 1877, p 59
[10] *Metropolitan Tabernacle Pulpit*, 1892, p 461

was his, and I was buried with him. I wish it had been earlier still.' He was very nervous — 'as timid and timorous a youth as you might see' — and the minister asked him if he would conduct through the water the two women who were the first to be baptised, but Spurgeon was too afraid. He had never seen a baptism before and was wary of making a mistake. Then it was his turn: 'The wind blew down the river with a cutting blast as my turn came to wade into the flood, but after I had walked a few steps, and noted the people on the ferry-boat and in boats, and on either shore, I felt as if heaven, and earth, and hell, might gaze upon me, for I was not ashamed, there and then, to own myself a follower of the Lamb. My timidity was washed away ... I have never felt anything of the kind since. Baptism also loosed my tongue ... I lost a thousand fears in that river Lark, and found that in keeping his commandments there is great reward'.[11] The following Sunday he sat down at the Lord's Table for the first time.

2.6   The Preaching School-Teacher

Four months after his baptism Spurgeon went as a teacher to a school in Cambridge where he remained for three years, without salary, receiving his board and lodging free. He became a member of the St Andrew's Street Baptist Church and was soon teaching a class in the Sunday School. A deacon named James Vinter organised a rota of preachers to supply small country churches, and hearing Spurgeon teaching his Sunday School class recruited him to his list. One Sunday afternoon he went to the village of Teversham accompanying a friend whom he thought was to preach on that occasion. On their journey they came to the agonising discovery that each had believed the other to be the appointed preacher. It was Spurgeon who asked God for help and in the gathering in the thatched cottage preached for the first time on I Peter 2:7, 'Unto you therefore which believe, he is precious.' He reported to his family, 'It was not half such a task as I feared it would be.'

When he finished preaching and was picking up the hymn-book to announce the closing hymn a woman's voice from the congregation broke the silence: "Bless your dear heart, how old are you?" Spurgeon looked gravely in that direction: "You must wait until the service is over before making any such enquiries. Let us now sing."

---

[11] *The Early Years*, p 149

The questioner was not easily silenced and after the service, repeated the question. "I am under sixty," said Spurgeon. "Yes, and under sixteen," replied the woman. "Never mind," said Spurgeon, "think of the Lord Jesus and his preciousness."

These were years when Spurgeon went to hear the leading preachers in the country. William Jay of Bath came to Cambridge shortly before his death on December 27th 1853 in his 85th year. He had been pastor of the Argyle Chapel for sixty-two years. John Newton and William Romaine had heard him preach, and Jay knew William Wilberforce and had also had a meal with John Wesley in 1789. Spurgeon heard him speak on the text, 'Let your conversation be as it becometh the gospel of Christ' and was impressed with his dignity and simplicity. Spurgeon also saved up to travel to Birmingham to hear John Angell James preaching. It was a mid-week service and James was preaching on, 'Ye are complete in him.' Some years later Spurgeon told him that he had gone to hear him, and that that had been his text. "Ah ! That was a Calvinistic sermon. You would enjoy that, but you would not get on with me always," he said.

2.7   The Waterbeach Pastor

In October 1851 Spurgeon preached for the first time at Waterbeach, a village a few miles outside Cambridge. Soon that church had called him to be its minister, and in January 1852 he commenced his pastorate there. He was 16 years of age and he continued there for 2 years. The first night he spent there he shared a bed with another boy. Spurgeon kneeled down and prayed before getting into bed, and then asked his companion if he were not afraid to go to sleep without asking God to protect him through the night. They talked together for an hour or two until they both kneeled down and prayed together. It was the beginning of salvation for the boy — who later was to become deacon Smith in the church.

Spurgeon immediately showed his ability to help people in spiritual perplexities, which factor is found in all his sermons. There was a woman at Waterbeach who totally lacked an assurance of salvation. She loved to come to the church, and to worship God. She could not stop away, but she confessed that she had no hope of heaven: "I do not believe it for myself," she said: "I am afraid whether it is for me." "Have you no hope at all?" asked Spurgeon. "None," she replied. So Spurgeon pulled out his wallet. "I have here £5. It is all the money

I've got, and I will give it to you for your hope, if you will sell it to me." She looked scornfully at the teenager. "I would not sell it for a thousand worlds," she said. In one sentence she was professing to have no hope of salvation and in the next that she would not part with it for anything!

It was during this time that he was advised to study at the Baptist College of Stepney (now Regent's Park, Oxford) and an appointment was made for him to meet with its principal, Dr Angus, at the Cambridge home of Mr MacMillan, the publisher (grandfather of Harold MacMillan, the late Prime Minister). A maid showed him into one room without informing the family that he had arrived, while they entertained Dr Angus in another room. After a long wait the principal left and then Spurgeon emerged from his room announcing that he was constrained to return to his school, to be told by the embarrassed MacMillans of the mistake.

This misunderstanding was borne with equanimity by Spurgeon. Within a month of the commencement of his ministry at Waterbeach (January 1852) the congregation had grown to 450 people and they loved their pastor. Numbers could not get in to the church. The deacons were delighted that he was not going off to college. The following year he wrote to his aunt: 'I am called "the boy preacher" or more commonly "the lad" ... I am 18 tomorrow and hope Sunday to preach for the 188th time since I started about one and a half years ago. This is the great object of my life. I don't want to be anything but a preacher of the gospel.'

2.8   The Call To London

In 1853 Spurgeon was asked to give an address at the annual meeting of the Cambridge Sunday School Union in the town's Guildhall. It was an extraordinary meeting. Three speakers were to give addresses and as Spurgeon was by far the youngest he spoke first of all and in his customary direct and profound manner. The other two speakers were both angry with this upstart, one of them in particular referred to his youth and said to the congregation that it was a pity that boys did not adopt the Scriptural practice of tarrying in Jericho till their beards were grown before they tried to instruct their seniors.

Spurgeon received permission from the chairman to return to the stage and reminded the audience that those who were bidden to tarry in Jericho were not boys, but full-grown men, whose beards had been shaved off by their enemies as the greatest indignity they could be made to suffer, and who were ashamed to return home until their beards had grown again. Then he paused and went on, saying that the parallel to this case would be that of a minister who fell into open sin and had disgraced his calling and needed to go into seclusion until his character was to some extent restored.

The young man was not to know what many in the congregation were aware of, that this preacher who had belittled him was in that exact condition. A solemnity quickly followed the tide of sympathy which had engulfed the meeting and one member of the audience in particular became very thoughtful. His name was George Gould and he resolved to give the news of this impressive young preacher to his close friend, Thomas Olney, a deacon of the New Park Street Chapel in Southwark, London. This well-known church was seeking a pastor. It had had some famous ministers in its time. Benjamin Keach had been one of its early pastors in the late seventeenth century. Dr. John Gill had preached there from 1719 and had remained for over fifty years (in 1852 Spurgeon had become a subscriber to a new edition of Gill's Commentary as it appeared in monthly parts). Dr John Rippon had also been a preacher there for sixty-three years until his death 18 years earlier (Spurgeon was using his hymn-book, Rippon's Selection, in Waterbeach). Both Gill and Rippon had commenced their ministries there at 19 years of age.

It was while Spurgeon was sitting in the Waterbeach 'big seat' a few weeks later preparing himself for the Sunday morning service that a letter was passed on to him and he opened it with curiosity. The letter was an invitation to fill the New Park Street pulpit as soon as possible. A stunned young preacher passed the letter on to another deacon and said that there must be a mistake. The man gravely shook his head, sensing the days of Spurgeon remaining in Waterbeach were numbered. The following day Spurgeon replied to Thomas Olney, 'My last birthday was only my nineteenth,' he wrote, 'and if you think my years would unqualify me for your pulpit, then do not let me come.' But he offered New Park Street a Sunday in the next month, December 11th, and that was duly accepted.

It was in a boarding-house in Bloomsbury that Spurgeon spent his Saturday night, sharing it with some young Anglicans who were tickled at this country preacher coming to speak at the New Park Street pulpit. They told him of the vast congregations and the matchless oratory of the preachers who had been at that chapel so that through the night Spurgeon was a very worried man (New Park Street was never to send a visiting preacher to a boarding house again).

Spurgeon walked through the cold streets of London that Sabbath morning as apprehensive as he had ever been in his life and the one verse of Scripture that kept coming to him was, 'He must needs go through Samaria.' But his day was a happy one: the congregation was small and he did not feel out of his depth and fellowship with warm-hearted members of the church encouraged him. He walked back to Bloomsbury that night feeling that he was not alone, and Londoners were not 'flinty-hearted barbarians'.

An invitation to return was immediately given to him. This was encouraging, as the church had had a succession of orthodox Baptist preachers occupying the pulpit and they had all proved to be uniformly dry men not welcomed back to New Park Street. They told Spurgeon that he was the only one they had heard with pleasure. Older members told him he reminded them of Dr Rippon. He replied that they did not know what they were doing, nor whether they were in the body or out of the body! He judged that they had been so starved that a morsel of gospel was a treat to them. In the 18 years since the death of John Rippon they had had three short pastorates, including Joseph Angus who had failed to meet with Spurgeon in the MacMillan household in Cambridge, and the congregation was shrinking. It was the largest Baptist chapel in Britain, a smoke-blackened building, situated south of the Thames accessible via a toll bridge. The area was low and flooded easily, while soot and stench was everywhere. Around the chapel stood a brewery, warehouses and factories. The only nearby houses were slums. Within a year an outbreak of Asiatic cholera raged through the district and night and day Spurgeon was to visit these homes, pray, read scripture and bury the dead.

On the Monday before returning to Cambridge Spurgeon climbed to the top of St. Paul's and then proceeded to a bookseller's where he spent the money New Park Street had given him in purchasing Thomas Scott's Commentary on the Bible.

On the Sundays January 1st, 15th and 29th in 1854 Spurgeon preached in the London church but before the third Sunday he was told that a full vestry of church members had voted to invite him to fill the pulpit for six months, only five people voting against him. Spurgeon replied on the day he received the letter accepting the call, but stipulating the time of probation be brought down to a three month period. But by April he had received a plea to become their pastor and again he quickly accepted this invitation. There was no ordination service; no so-called 'area-superintendent' had to be present to validate this bond between hungry sheep and caring shepherd. The work was recognised by the rush of people that filled the building every Sunday. Spurgeon allowed the title 'Reverend' to be used for 11 years, but after that was known simply as 'pastor'. He wore no clerical gown except on one occasion in his life when he was 26 and he preached in Calvin's pulpit in Geneva. He said that he would have worn the pope's tiara to have had the honour of preaching there.

2.9   The New Park Street Ministry

Within twelve weeks every seat in New Park Street Chapel was taken. There was no advertising whatsoever in these early days. The members of the congregation who heard him told their friends (without having been exhorted to do so) with the deepest earnestness of the benefit they received from this ministry and many who heard these things resolved to come themselves. They were to return the next weeks bringing others. In fact New Park Street chapel could be used thus for just one year. In the following February the congregation met for two months at Exeter Hall in the Strand while New Park Street was being enlarged. Exeter Hall was a building which was used for religious meetings but was generally used by the Sacred Harmonic Society. It was capable of holding from 4,000 to 5,000 persons. Then the congregation returned to New Park Street for another year, before the pressure of numbers made them return again to the Exeter Hall in June 1856 for four more months. By this time they had given in to the inevitable and were planning a new building.

We know exactly what these vast congregations saw and heard, and in the most comprehensive manner, because from almost the very beginning Spurgeon's sermons were taken down in short-hand and printed. We have 53 sermons from his first complete calendar year at the church, the New Park Street Pulpit 1855. We can read his sermon, for example, of January 7 on 'The Immutability of God' on the text, 'I am the Lord, I change not; therefore ye sons of Jacob are not consumed,' Malachi 3:6. Spurgeon was 20 years and 6 months old, and this is how he began his 45 minute sermon:

> It has been said by some one that, 'the proper study
> of mankind is man.' I will not oppose the idea, but I
> believe it is equally true that the proper study of God's

elect is God; the proper study of a Christian is the God-head. The highest science, the loftiest speculation, the mightiest philosophy, which can ever engage the attention of a child of God, is the name, the nature, the person, the work, the doings, and the existence of the great God whom he calls his Father. There is something exceedingly improving to the mind in a contemplation of the Divinity. It is a subject so vast, that all our thoughts are lost in its immensity; so deep, that our pride is drowned in its infinity. Other subjects we can compass and grapple with; in them we feel a kind of self-content, and go our way with the thought, 'Behold I am wise.' But when we come to this master-science, finding that our plumb-line cannot sound its depth, and that our eagle eye cannot see its height, we turn away with the thought, that vain man would be wise, but he is like a wild ass's colt; and with the solemn exclamation, 'I am but of yesterday, and know nothing.' No subject of contemplation will tend more to humble the mind than thoughts of God. We shall be obliged to feel

Great God, how infinite art thou,
What worthless worms are we!

Spurgeon's sermons, from the very beginning, have all the qualities of the greatest preachers in the history of the church. They are authoritative, God-centred and cross-centred, profound, creative, with newly-minted phraseology, ardent and full of pastoral application. They home in on the consciences of non-Christians and they are focused upon the affections of those who are believers to move them to trust and adore. Within a year Spurgeon was completely at home in the New Park Street pulpit. He could be relaxed while consumed by his themes, and would unite a congregation into that intent listening which stirred them to inward consecration or confession or thanksgiving or concern, as one such affectionate response to the Word would hurry on the steps of another. Reading his New Park Street sermons today there are all those elements of authority, integrity and depth which make it difficult to conceive that they are coming from a self-taught man not yet 21 years of age.

We also know how he prayed in the pulpit in those early years because some of his prayers were also stenographically recorded. On

Tuesday night, December 31, 1855, at a Watch-Night Service Spurgeon prayed:

> O God, save my people. Save my people. A solemn charge hast thou given to thy servant. Ah, Lord, it is all too solemn for such a child. Help him. Help him by thine own grace to discharge it as he ought. O Lord, let thy servant confess that he feels that his prayers are not as earnest as they should be for his people's souls; that he does not preach so frequently as he ought, with that fire, that energy, that true love to men's souls. But O Lord, damn not the hearers for the preacher's sin. O, destroy not the flock for the shepherd's iniquity. Have mercy on them, good Lord, have mercy on them. O Lord, have mercy on them! There are some of them, Father, that will not have mercy on themselves. How have we preached to them, and laboured for them. O God thou knowest that I lie not. How have I striven for them, that they might be saved. But the heart is too hard for man to melt and the soul made of iron too hard for flesh and blood to render soft. O God, the God of Israel, thou canst save.[12]

And so on, for as long again, of such heart-breaking expressions of spontaneous devotion to God and of love for those he was praying for. One would make the judgment that not since the apostles had there been such pulpit prayers. Twenty-six of *CH Spurgeon's Prayers*, under that title, were published in 1905 and are still in print (Pilgrim Publications, USA). Who talked with God as Spurgeon did?

2.10   A Typical Sunday Service

We also are aware of the whole structure of his Sunday services. We have a description from an anonymous observer who wrote a little book on church leaders of the 19th century entitled *Teachers and Preachers.* He recounted:

'The hall became speedily full to its utmost capacity. Mr. Spurgeon opened the service by a brief prayer. Then, upon his invitation, the whole congregation rose and with hearty goodwill sang "All people that on earth do dwell," to Old Hundredth. There is no organ

---

[12] *New Park Street Pulpit*, 1856, p 43

there, a gentleman stepping forward from Mr Spurgeon's side and raising the tune. But after the first note of the first verse his voice was heard no more, being lost in the mighty sound of thousands of voices that rolled forth the familiar tune. After this Mr Spurgeon read a portion of the eleventh chapter of Matthew. The reading of what elsewhere would be called the lesson was accompanied by a running commentary of homely explanation and earnest exhortation. Another hymn, a second and longer prayer and then Mr Spurgeon began to preach to the manifestly interested crowd.

'Spurgeon took as his text the three last verses of the chapter which he had read, and spoke about it in a simple and at times passionately earnest manner for the space of fifty minutes. "Come unto me, all ye that labour and are heavy laden, and I will give you rest", was the burden of the text, and the preacher was content with reiterating and varying this invitation, insisting on the illimitability of the proffered welcome, and dwelling on the perfection of the promised rest. Twice only did he vary his discourse by the introduction of illustrations in parable form, which he is much accustomed to use for the enforcement of his text.

'One of these was short and contained within itself the main argument of the discourse. "There is a doctor who visits you," he said. "You have called him in because you are feeling very ill and the first thing he says to you is, "Do you trust me entirely?" You say, "Oh, yes, doctor, I trust you entirely." "Very well; now tell me what you eat and what you drink." You tell him, and he declares that you are eating and drinking the very things that feed your disease. He tells you you must give up those things, and asks you if you will take some medicine he will send you. Oh, yes, you will do everything he tells you, and he goes away.

'A few days later he calls again, and finds you worse. "Why, how is this?" he says; "your disease is getting a firmer hold upon you." But when he comes to inquire, he finds that you have been going on eating and drinking the same things as before. "Did you take the medicine?" "Well," you say, "I just tasted it, but found it was nasty and there it is." Then the doctor knows that you have not trusted him, and he goes away sorrowful; for he knows that without that trust he can do you no good. It is just so with Jesus Christ. You must trust him entirely and do everything he tells you, for those are the sole conditions upon which he will give you rest.

'This was, in brief, the sermon. It was listened to throughout with never-faltering attention by the great congregation, to whom, seated or standing in whatever remote corner of the hall, the preacher's voice was as audible as if he were speaking to them across the table.'[13]

So the elements that constituted all Spurgeon's services were all those which were present in the New Testament church — the fervent love for God and for one another of a holy congregation of believers, prayer, psalms, hymns and spiritual songs, the reading of the Scriptures, preaching, the baptism of believers and the Lord's Supper (celebrated every Sunday morning). None of those elements absent from the New Testament had a place in his services: no organs and musical instruments, no drama, and certainly no dancing, even when there was this great moving of God's Spirit. Spurgeon said, 'When Christmas Evans preached in Wales, during a time of revival, he used to make the people dance,[14] the congregation were so excited under his ministry that they positively danced. Now I do not believe that dancing was the work of the Spirit. Their being stirred in their hearts might be the Holy Spirit's work, but the Holy Spirit does not care to make people dance under sermons; no good comes of it. Now and then among our Methodist friends there is a great break-out, and we hear of a young woman in the middle of a sermon getting on the top of a form and turning round and round in ecstasy, till she falls down in a fainting fit, and they cry, "Glory to God." Now we do not believe that that is the work of the Spirit; we believe it is ridiculous nonsense, and nothing more ...

'Even the great Whitefield's revival at Cambuslang, one of the greatest and most remarkable revivals that was ever known, was attended by some things that we cannot but regard as superstitious wonders. People were so excited, that they did not know what they did. Now, if in any revival you see any of these strange contortions of the body, always distinguish between things that differ. The Holy Spirit's work is with the mind, not with the body in that way. It is not the will of God that such things should disgrace the proceedings. I believe that such things are the result of Satanic malice. The devil sees that there is a great deal of good doing; "Now," says he, "I'll spoil it all. I'll put my hoof in there, and do a world of mischief. There are souls being converted; I will let them get so excited that they will do ludicrous things, and then it will all be brought into contempt."

'Now if you see any of these strange works arising, look out.

---

[13] *Teachers and Preachers*, pp 144–5

[14] This is hard to believe. We know that Spurgeon personally supported Christmas Evans's widow for many years

There is that old Apolyon busy, trying to mar the work. Put such va-
garies down as soon as you can, for where the Spirit works, he never
works against his own precept, and his precept is, "Let all things be
done decently and in order." It is neither decent nor orderly for
people to dance under the sermon, nor howl, nor scream, while the
gospel is being preached to them, and therefore it is not the Spirit's
work at all, but mere human excitement.'[15]

2.11   The Impression Spurgeon Made

The impression Spurgeon made was not always initially favourable
on those who became his greatest supporters. His wife was perplexed
by him when she first heard him. The Archbishop of Canterbury un-
fortunately committed to writing in his diary this comment (which
seems to have overtones of professional jealousy), 'Mr Spurgeon is
certainly uglier than I had believed.' He later became one of Spurgeon's strongest admirers and prayed at his funeral service. Spurgeon was variously described as a 'hair-dresser's assistant' or, more
typically, 'a gentleman farmer on holiday.' But as the years went by
he was generally viewed as the archetypal Englishman, Mr. John
Bull.

The novelist George Eliot, no friend of evangelical religion,
wrote that he had 'a gift of a fine voice, very flexible and various,
admirably clear and fluent in his language, but common and empty
of guiding intelligence.' John Ruskin, who much admired him said,
'very wonderful . . . there is always in Spurgeon's sermons at least one
passage which no other man in London could have given.'

The most interesting response to Spurgeon is that of Charles
Greville who was at the Music Hall, Royal Surrey Gardens, on Sunday morning February 8, 1857 and heard the 23 year-old Spurgeon
preach to 9,000 people on Psalm 19, verse 12; 'Cleanse thou me from
secret faults.'[16]   Greville noticed that John Ruskin was also there.
The sermon comes to a thrilling conclusion with one of those unique
passages which Ruskin had noted:

---

[15] *The Great Revival*, a sermon on Isaiah 52:10; 'The Lord hath made bare his holy
arm in the eyes of all the nations; and all the ends of the earth shall see the salvation
of our God.' This sermon was preached on Sunday March 28, 1858 in the Music Hall,
Surrey Gardens, and is to be found in *New Park Street Pulpit*, 1858, p 161ff

[16] The sermon is to be found in *New Park Street Pulpit*, 1857, p 73ff

'When Christ comes a second time, there will be a
marvellous change in the way men talk. Methinks I see
him; there he sits upon his throne. Now, Caiaphas, come
and condemn him now! Judas! come and kiss him now!
What do you stick at man? Are you afraid of him? Now
Barabbas! Go! See whether they will prefer you to Christ
now. Swearer, now is your time; you have been a bold
man; curse him to his face now. Now drunkard; stagger
up to him now. Now infidel; tell him there is no Christ
now — now that the world is lit with lightning and the
earth is shaken with thunder till the solid pillars thereof
do bow themselves — tell God there is no God now; now
laugh at the Bible; now scoff at the minister. Why men,
what is the matter with you? Why can't you do it? Ah!
there you are; you have fled to the hills and to the rocks
— "Rocks hide us! Mountains fall on us! Hide us from
the face of him that sitteth on the throne." Ah! Where
are now your boasts, your vaunting, and your glories?
Alas! Alas! for you in that dread day of wonders.'

Charles Greville was then 63 years of age. He was the grandson
of Lord Warwick, a former Eton scholar and page to George III. He
was a race-horse owner and a cynic. His friend and biographer Sir
Henry Taylor described him as 'high born, high bred, avowedly Epi-
curean.' Yet the *Dictionary of National Biography* judges him to be
'one of the most remarkable men of his generation.' For forty years
he kept a diary with great pains, assessing and correcting what he
had written with as much neutrality and good judgment as he was
capable. This diary is described in the above dictionary as the 'most
important work of its kind' especially because of its many brilliant
portraits of European leaders whom Greville observed.

In what words did Greville record his impression of that perora-
tion of Spurgeon? He wrote the following appreciation: 'I have just
heard the celebrated Mr. Spurgeon in Surrey Gardens on; "Cleanse
me from my secret sins" (*sic*). He is certainly very remarkable, and
undeniably a fine character; not remarkable in person, and in face
rather resembling a smaller Macaulay, a very clear and powerful
voice, which was heard through the whole hall: a manner natural,
impassioned, and without affectation or extravagance; wonderful flu-
ency and command of language, abounding in illustration, and very
often of a familiar kind, but without anything either ridiculous or ir-

reverent. He gave me an impression of his earnestness and sincerity, speaking without books or notes, yet the discourse was evidently very carefully prepared.'

On another occasion Spurgeon was heard by the Scottish minister and social reformer, Thomas Guthrie of Free St John's, Edinburgh (now known as Free St. Columba's). Guthrie wrote, There were as usual a great crowd — some 6,000 or 7,000 people and we had a good sermon. We went into the vestry after the service and had a crack with the greatest of English preachers. Had he more of the emotional, great as he is, he would be still greater. He was very genial and kind.' Guthrie had the ability to dissolve a congregation into tears, and judged this to be the mark of great preaching. Spurgeon, no doubt, was not lacking in such a facility, but that ambition never entered his mind. He judged tears or laughter to be amongst the most rudimentary responses for any preacher to create and to have little to do with the presence of the Spirit of God, or in encouraging Christ-likeness.

Alongside this good-natured observation and comment went the most cruel character assassinations a London preacher has ever had to endure. Men hated Spurgeon both within and outside of the professing church. James Wells, the hyper-Calvinist, and self-appointed keeper of orthodoxy in England, wrote in *The Earthern Vessel*, January 1855, 'I have — most solemnly have — my doubts as to the Divine reality of his conversion.' In the next month the *Ipswich Express* reported Spurgeon as having said before his sermon, "as there are many young ladies present, I want them to know that I am engaged. My heart is another's, and I want you to clearly understand that I will have no presents sent to me, no attention paid, and no worsted slippers worked for me by the women present." The following week they printed an apology, but the report had been reprinted in other papers and would not die. Then in April the reporter of the *Essex Standard* judged Spurgeon thus: 'His style is that of the vulgar colloquial, varied by rant ... All the most solemn mysteries of our holy religion are by him rudely, roughly and impiously handled. Common sense is outraged and decency disgusted. His rantings are interspersed with coarse anecdotes.' A long attack in the *Sheffield and Rotherham Independent* contained the opinion, 'He is a nine days' wonder — a comet that has suddenly shot across the religious atmosphere. He has gone up like a rocket and ere long will come down like a stick.' The first scrap-book which his wife kept bulged with press criticisms like the above from the years 1855 and 1856.

It is certainly true that this manner of directly confronting people with the gospel of Jesus Christ had disappeared from English
churches. A reporter observed, 'Spurgeon speaks to the people not
in the language of books, but in their own language.' More than that,
he spoke with his distinct Essex accent. Words that ended on 'ah' or
'oh' he pronounced 'er'. Thus 'Noah' became 'Nore,' and 'poor' became 'pore.' Part of his directness came from the anti-ornateness of
his style: 'I have said "damn" where God said "damn". I have not
sweetened it into "condemn."'

'Do not be squeamish in the pulpit,' he told his students, like one
who read, 'Jonah was 3 days and 3 nights in the ... ahem, society of
the fish'. Spurgeon said, 'Soft speaking for soft heads, and good plain
speech for the hard-headed many. Mincing words and pretty sentences are for those who wear kid-gloves and eye-glasses.' Certainly
Spurgeon never made the Word of God seem boring: 'Dull preachers
make good martyrs. They are so dry they burn well.'

Yet he was not the impetuous and thoughtless preacher others
suggested. When Randall Davidson, the future Archbishop of Canterbury, went to hear him preach, during the week preceding that
Sunday the *Pall Mall Gazette* had published a notorious exposé of the
white slave trade, which became the sensation of London. Davidson
feared Spurgeon might preach a sensationalist sermon on this subject, but, according to Davidson, 'he did not say one word which was
indiscreet or coarse or harmful.'

There was more editing done to all his later sermons. 'The earlier sermons ... owing to my constant wanderings abroad, received
scarcely any revision and consequently they abound in colloquialisms
and other offenses.'[17] According to the short-hand secretary who
kept the record of his sermons Spurgeon spoke, on average, one hundred and forty words per minute. His account was lengthened or cut
to meet publishers' requirements and in the last years of his life he
passed the job of revision on to W Y Fullerton, who frequently ex-
panded the seven pages of notes to twelve pages of text for publication, removing the spontaneity and roughness.[18]

To hear the authentic Spurgeon nothing compares with the 6 volumes of the virtually unedited *New Park Street Pulpit.* And yet the
most significant fact of all is the consistency of the sermons throughout his ministry. An acquaintance once told him that the sermons

---

[17] *The Autobiography,* II, p 158
[18] *C H Spurgeon, A Biography,* W Y Fullerton, London, 1920, p 218

of the first ten years of his ministry in London and the sermons of
the last decade of his life were his best and that there seems to have
been a comparative sag in the middle decade when the Metropolitan
Tabernacle opened. And Spurgeon agreed with that. His best writing
to convict and elevate preachers is his incomparable *An All Round
Ministry.*

2.12 The Impression Spurgeon's Congregation Made

Every great preacher has a great congregation. The one always com-
plements and fires the other. Although, as in this century, the pattern in the 19th Century was for more women than men to attend
church, in Spurgeon's congregation the men predominated. At the
very beginning Edmund Fry, who wrote the first of Spurgeon's biographies (when the preacher was approaching his 21st birthday),
acknowledged this. Spurgeon himself said, 'nine-tenths of my hearers are men.' He felt that one reason was the awful crush of people
pressing in to attend the services: 'Women cannot endure this awful pressure, the rending of the clothes and so on.' A visitor to the
Metropolitan Tabernacle twenty years later also noted that this was
a predominantly masculine congregation; 'men of solid sense and intelligence.'

Spurgeon's critics described his audience as consisting of prosperous non-conformist tradesmen. An Anglican paper reported that
they occupied 'the social zone between the mechanic and the successful, but not fashionable, tradesman.' Charles Booth wrote, 'The congregation consists of middle-class, chiefly lower-middle-class people
— for the most part comfortable, successful, godly folk. It is not to
any considerable extent a working-class body.' *The Times* reported
the victims of the Surrey Music Hall disaster as being 'respectably
dressed — a respectable boy of 13, a 26 year-old workman, a maid-
servant and a couple of housewives.'

Yet there were others from another strata in society who were
church-members. His brother James, who became his assistant, married the daughter of Lord John Burgoyne, the Constable of the Tower
of London. Spurgeon often mentions the Burgoyne family being
prominent members of the congregation. Everyone was drawn to
hear Spurgeon: Lord John Russell, Lady Peel, Lord Shaftesbury,

Lord Campbell, the Archbishop of Canterbury, Florence Nightingale, George Eliot, Matthew Arnold, Gladstone (who sat in the pulpit behind him) and the young Lloyd-George on his honeymoon — all are recorded as having gone to hear him.

Spurgeon said, 'People come to me for one thing, and it is no use my pretending to give them the opposite as well. I preach to them a Calvinist creed and a Puritan morality. That is what they want and that is what they get. If they want anything else they must go elsewhere.' He said he was flattered when visitors grumbled because they detected nothing special in his preaching: 'The best style of preaching in the world, like the best style of dressing, is that which nobody notices.'

2.13   The Notable Year of 1856

1856 was a significant year in the life of Charles Haddon Spurgeon. Within one year almost everyone in London had come to hear of him. He was not 22 years of age until the month of June, but events, great and small, came hurtling toward him. Madame Tussaud erected a waxwork model of him in her Exhibition. Spurgeon began to instruct his first theological student, Thomas Medhurst and before long he was training eight men. But two events stood out: on January 8 he married Susannah Thompson. She had been present at the first Sunday evening service in New Park Street and had been amused by his enormous black satin cravat, badly-trimmed hair and blue handkerchief with white spots. She was the only child of a prosperous ribbon-manufacturer, a friend of the Olneys and so Spurgeon met her there often and within ten weeks had given her a copy of *Pilgrim's Progress*. They spoke of their love for one another at the opening ceremonies of the Crystal Palace, and in January 1855 he baptised her. A year later on January 8, 1856 they were married and took their honeymoon in Paris, where she had been many times before. Ten months after the wedding their twin sons were born. Soon afterwards Susannah became ill and for the rest of her marriage she was virtually bed-ridden. Charles had a desk built with extending arms on which note-paper and books could be kept, and from her bed she continued a notable ministry of letter-writing and book distribution. What was wrong with Susannah Spurgeon? Sir James Simpson was a friend of the Spurgeons (and also of Thomas Chalmers), an elder in the Scottish Free Church, discoverer of anæsthetic for operations and the father of modern gynæcology. In 1869 he performed an operation on Susannah. He normally charged £1,000 for an operation, but he told Spurgeon he could pay him when he became Archbishop of Canterbury. A clue to Susannah's illness is found in Spurgeon's personal library which has been located in the William Jewell College, Missouri, USA since 1905. There is one volume on the shelves which has a certain incongruity. It is entitled *A Practical Treatise on the Inflammation of the Uterus, the Cervix and on its Connections with other Uterine Diseases.* The operation was not a success and yet Susannah Spurgeon outlived him by ten years. Spurgeon had kidney disease. They were a sickly pair, but blissfully happy. He would send her a stream of cards, letters and love notes from all his travels. One from Pompei has this message scribbled on it, 'I send tons of love to you — hot as fresh lava.' If there was something she fancied, be it an opal ring or a bull-finch, he would get it for her.

2.14   The Surrey Gardens

The Surrey Gardens was a precursor of today's amusement parks. It contained a small zoo where children could purchase rides on a giant tortoise and there were elaborate fireworks displays (and soon one tableau was to feature the face of Spurgeon). The striking new feature at the centre of the Surrey Gardens was the erection of the largest Music Hall in the world. It held 10,000 people, and London buzzed with interest in it. With thousands being turned away from the Exeter Hall, Spurgeon decided to move to this Music Hall for his Sunday services. The decision was not without opposition: "Don't go and preach in the devil's house," said one of his deacons.

The first service there became the occasion of a famous tragedy. Crowds thronged the building for some hours before it opened. Twelve thousand squeezed in and several thousand more crowded around the exits. The audience settled down after the opening hymn, but in the prayer a noise and shouts were heard. Some thought they were cries of fire, while others thought they warned that the roof was falling in. There was a panic, and the 22 year-old Spurgeon imposed his considerable authority on the crowd crying, "Remain in your seats! Beware of pickpockets!" The crowd surging out met the throng of those packed around the entrances and in the crush seven people died and others were injured. But the congregation in front of the pulpit and Spurgeon himself were unaware of this tragedy.

A hymn was announced and when the congregation sat down some cried out to Spurgeon to preach. He announced a text from Proverbs 3:33, 'The curse of the Lord is in the house of the wicked.' He had barely begun to open up his theme when the wave of disorder became too distracting. Spurgeon dismissed the congregation and fainted. He was taken home and not immediately told the fact of the deaths. The next day the press censured him with little mercy, that he should have held a religious service in that building, that the deacons should have continued to take an offering while this was going on and that he should have carried on with the service. For some days Spurgeon was sick at heart and perplexed at what had happened. Subsequently he was even more fearful of crowds and packed buildings. But with his confidence restored through prayer, Spurgeon returned to the scene of the tragedy four weeks later and preached there for three more years to congregations of ten thousand people without incident.

Many of his sermons there were transcribed and are to be found in *New Park Street Pulpit*, Vol 2, no 104; through vol 6, no 289, which particular sermon is an account of his last message there, *The Minister's Farewell*, which is based on Paul's farewell to the Ephesian elders and was preached in December 1859. In the course of that sermon he said, 'I wish not to say anything in self-commendation and praise; I take you to witness this day, that I have not shunned to declare unto you all the counsel of God. Often have I come into this pulpit in great weakness and I have far more often gone away in great sorrow, because I have not preached to you as earnestly as I desired. I confess to many errors and failings and more especially to a want of earnestness when engaged in prayer for your souls. But there is one charge which my conscience acquits me of this morning and I think you will acquit me too, for I have not shunned to declare the whole counsel of God.' (p29)

The reason Spurgeon stopped using the Music Hall was as a protest against the owners who decided to open the amusement park on the Lord's Day. He went back to the Exeter Hall for two years until the opening of the Metropolitan Tabernacle.

2.15   The Metropolitan Tabernacle

The Metropolitan Tabernacle was opened in the spring of 1861, and was immediately called 'Spurgeon's Tabernacle.' Spurgeon was totally involved in the new building from its conception. His gifts of church administration were as magisterial as his pulpit ability. Spurgeon supervised every aspect of the new building, its name, site and design.

The name 'Tabernacle' was chosen because they were to be a pilgrim congregation in London. They were not interested in erecting a temple in the city. Spurgeon also decided on the site of the building on the convergence of six roads in Newington Butts opposite a well-known hostelry called the 'Elephant and Castle.' Unlike Westminster Chapel which is a stone's throw from Buckingham Palace and whose foundations were laid two years after the opening of Spurgeon's Tabernacle, this was not a central location. But Newington Butts was an area of potential growth south of the river Thames and not far from the original building in New Park Street. Spurgeon insisted the building be erected on a freehold site and though this required an act of Parliament, this was obtained.

Spurgeon also had convictions about the architecture of the building. He would consider only the Grecian style. The Victorian period, with the rise of the Oxford Movement, was characterised by a vogue for a return to Gothic architecture.[19] Churches of Gothic design were completely vaulted in stone with ribbed vaults, large areas of stained glass, pointed arches, buttresses, mouldings, carvings and ornamented furniture. The cathedrals of Salisbury, Lincoln and York Minster are typically Gothic of the 13th to 15th centuries. Pugin designed the Houses of Parliament in that style, and John Ruskin encouraged Spurgeon to go for a Gothic design for the Tabernacle: "That is the best expression of Christianity," he told him. Spurgeon gave that idea short shrift. For him Gothic was a return to the superstition of the Middle Ages. Greek was the Christian tongue; it was the language of the New Testament; it was the Baptist tongue. 'Every Baptist place of worship should be Grecian, never Gothic. We owe nothing to the Goths as religionists.'[20] So the Tabernacle was a Grecian design, its porch of six great pillars, echoing the Parthenon — the temple of Athene! That original façade, approved by Spurgeon, still stands today as the only part of the original design to have survived the fires of 1898 and 1941.

In 1861, the Metropolitan Tabernacle was the largest non-conformist Christian building to have been erected, to hold the largest

---

[19] *cf* A C Pugin's *Specimens of Gothic Architecture*, 1825, and A W Pugin's *Glossary of Ecclesiastical Ornament and Costume*, 1868)

[20] Curiously Pugin and Ruskin, who both professed the Christian faith, ended their days in a mental asylum.

congregation in the history of the church until that time. It was well designed. There was the vast floor level (referred to as 'the Area') and two galleries. There was seating for 3,600 people. At the ends of the pews were flap seats, which, when lifted into position (held by iron rods) could seat another thousand. Besides this, there was standing room for a further thousand people, so that 6,000 people could hear the 26 year-old preacher. Stairways and exits provided speedy exit from the building in case of an emergency.

A curved platform projected from the front of the first gallery containing a desk and a settee. At the back was a row of chairs for the deacons. Below this pulpit was the marble baptistry over which for the weekly celebration of the Lord's Supper on Sunday mornings a platform was placed upon which the communion table and chairs were set.

People who wished to attend regularly paid for a seat on a three-monthly basis and were admitted by ticket. Others remained outside until five minutes before the beginning of the service, at which time they were allowed to take any empty seats. The rent from the 3,000 pew holders constituted the Tabernacle's chief income. There was no offering taken during the service. Spurgeon took no salary, living on the royalties from his publications. He had an annual income for £20,000 to £30,000 but was exceptionally generous and maintained his various ministries, leaving an estate of a mere £2,000 at the end of his life. It is known that there was a box near the entrance of the building to receive gifts for the support of the College, and there may well have been other boxes for gifts for the general support of the church.

The Metropolitan Tabernacle's opening services began on Monday, March 18, 1861 with a 7 a.m. prayer meeting which was attended by 1000 people and they ended on Thursday, April 11, with a day conference of speakers preaching on the 'Five Points of Calvinism.'

2.16   A Local Church

There is no way that a great preacher in a central location can escape a large floating congregation, and to that measure such churches are preaching centres. Yet by constant endeavour the congregation at Metropolitan Tabernacle were reminded that they were workers in a local church. There was, as has been noted, the service of holy communion every Sunday morning. This was open to every Christian.

Spurgeon said, 'Every man who became a member of a recognised Church of Christ had a perfect right to Christian ordinances, he had a right to baptism and the Lord's Supper, and the fact of a man's being unbaptised, was no reason why he should not have extended to him the fullest Christian fellowship.' Yet membership of the Tabernacle was restricted to those who had been baptised on profession of faith. Spurgeon again said that he 'would rather give up his pastorate than admit any man to the church who was not obedient to his Lord's command.'[21] There were about 40 baptisms a month.

Spurgeon personally interviewed every applicant for membership. He once told his congregation, 'I lately saw forty persons one by one and listened to their experiences and proposed them to the church. I felt as weary as ever a man did in reaping the harvest. I did not merely give them a few words as enquirers, but examined them as candidates with my best judgment. I thought that if I had many days of that sort I must die, but I also wished it may be my lot to die in that fashion.'[22]

There were also on average two deaths amongst the church members each week and we find Spurgeon speaking to the congregation and saying, 'I suppose, according to the natural order of things, two of you must die each week and when I think of this solemn fact I ask — where are the two? Where are the two who are to be the victims of death this week?'[23]

In 1866 *Our Own Hymn-Book* appeared. Until that time they had used two hymn books, Dr Rippon's *Selection* and Isaac Watt's *Psalms and Hymns.* There were problems with having two books, compounded by the fact that Rippon's *Selection* was divided up into many parts while Watts' work consisted of three books. Strangers in the congregation were often nonplussed finding the correct hymn. Spurgeon noted this with growing irritation: 'Many a time we marked their futile researches and pitied the looks of despair with which they have given up all hope of finding the hymns and so of joining intelligently in our words of praise.'[24] Spurgeon had worked on compiling this new selection of hymns for some years and soon it was adopted by hundreds of other congregations. Like every preacher Spurgeon had convictions on what was the best hymnology. *Our Own Hymn-Book* began with paraphrases of the 150 Psalms. There were seven selec-

[21] *Metropolitan Tabernacle Pulpit,* 1861, p 260

[22] *Metropolitan Tabernacle Pulpit,* 1884, p 310

[23] *Metropolitan Tabernacle Pulpit,* 1863, p 444

[24] Preface to *Our Own Hymn-Book*

tions of Psalm 119 all numbered '119.' Some of the paraphrases were written by Spurgeon and the book contains his little-known grace to be sung before a meal:

> *Heavenly Father, grant Thy blessing*
> *On the food before us spread.*
> *All our tongues are now confessing,*
> *By Thy hand alone we're fed,*
> *And Thou givest,*
> *Best of all, the living bread.*
> *(No 1056)*

But there were significant omissions. Neither, 'I asked the Lord that I might grow ...', nor ''Tis a point I long to know ...', were included. Concerning the omission of the latter, Spurgeon wrote, 'I deliberated a good deal about it, and I left it out not because I doubt whether a Christian may sing it, not because I have not sung it myself, but because I am not quite clear that I ought to ask any congregation to sing it; for I hope that most of those in ordinary congregations will not be in such a state of mind as that. Chronic doubt is a sin that is not to be tolerated.'[25]

When Sankey's Sacred Songs and Solos appeared in Britain in 1882 and swept through the country Spurgeon welcomed it without enthusiasm. He wrote in the *Sword and Trowel* that it might be acceptable for enlivening a weekly prayer meeting but that it was not suitable for Sunday services. Ira D Sankey was to sing at Spurgeon's funeral service, though Spurgeon could have no control over that.

2.17   Church Activities

One thousand children came to the Sunday School which was held in the Tabernacle and in the College. One adult class was presided over for many years by a Mrs Bartlett and between 500 and 700 people attended. After her death her son Edward maintained its testimony. Through it many people became church members. It organised evangelism and the dispossessed were visited and helped. Its members raised a large sum of money each year in support of the College. A Mr Perkins organised a large class of young men which met on Sunday afternoon in the Tabernacle vestry. There were similar classes run by a Mr Bowker and a Mr Charlesworth.

---

[25] *Metropolitan Tabernacle Pulpit*, 1906, p 490

There was a Building Fund which gave loans to chapels in debt. A German Mission supported two missionaries in Germany. Four large London missions were maintained by the church. There was a mission to the blind of London. About seventy poor women of the area were supported by the 'Mothers' Mission'. A 'Baptist Country Mission' maintained evangelism in country villages and several churches were started as a result of this work. There was also an 'Evangelists' Association' and another ministry of mercy to the poor entitled the 'Ordinance Poor Fund'. This is only a small selection of the work done by church members.

2.18   Spurgeon's Praying

A book containing transcriptions of Spurgeon's pulpit prayers was published in 1905 and it has been reprinted by Pilgrim Publications. Dr John Cairns once said that much as he rejoiced in Spurgeon's sermons he rejoiced yet more in his prayers. They are breath-takingly creative and spontaneous outbursts of a heart inflamed with love for God. The famous Methodist preacher, Dinsdale T Young, once heard Spurgeon say, 'O God, if some of us began to doubt thee we should begin to doubt our senses, for thou hast done such wonderful things for us. Thou has done more for us than thou didst for Thomas. Thou didst allow Thomas to thrust his finger into thy wounds; but thou hast often thrust thy finger into our wounds, and healed them.'

Spurgeon's prayers were full of theology: 'Beware of an untheological devotion,' he would warn. There was care shown in acknowledging the differences in the persons and work of the members of the Godhead. He had studied God, delighted in God and walked with God, especially the Son of God. The blood of the everlasting covenant was everything to his devotion.

Speaking of leading the Metropolitan Tabernacle congregation in prayer he said, 'The happiest moments of my life are those spent on this spot where I'm now standing. I have experienced more true happiness on this platform than I could have enjoyed on any other place on the face of the earth. I know that I have seemed to have been in the immediate presence of God while I have been leading you in supplication.'[26] Yet he also acknowledged the difficulty he experienced in the public prayer: 'I usually feel more dissatisfied with

---

[26] *Metropolitan Tabernacle Pulpit,* 1902, p 186

my prayers than with anything else I do.'[27]

Spurgeon was critical of those ministers of the 17th Century whose public prayers lasted three-quarters of an hour, or even an hour and a half. "I do not like that," he said.[28] His own prayers lasted from 10 to 12 minutes and to justify that brevity he appealed to the Scriptures where the longest recorded prayer would take about 6 minutes to repeat.[29] 'It is not necessary in prayer to rehearse the Westminster Assembly's Catechism,' he said.[30]

The importance of the public prayer in his estimation can be gleaned from his *Lectures to My Students*, where the fourth lecture is given over to that theme. He exhorted his men to avoid what he called 'an unhallowed and sickening superabundance of endearing words.' He urged them to vary the length of their public prayers and the current of their praying. Preachers should avoid all attempts to work up spurious fervour in public devotion. 'Let your prayers be earnest, full of fire, vehemence, prevalence,' he said[31] and that is how he himself prayed.

Spurgeon also taught that the best preparation for any public ministry was the discipline of private devotions: 'How dare we pray in the battle if we have never cried to the Lord while buckling on our armour!' he said to his students. He admired much the intense prolonged times of personal devotion of Alleine, Martyn and Brainerd —'You cannot pray too long in private. The more you are on your knees alone the better,' he would say.

Spurgeon lived with an awareness that he could only survive by God's help: 'I always feel that there is something wrong if I go without prayer for even half an hour in the day.'[32] Yet he also commended succinct and pointed praying: 'When I pray, I like to go to God just as I go to a bank clerk when I have a cheque to be cashed. I walk in, put the cheque down on the counter, the clerk gives me my money, I take it up, and go about my business. I do not know that I ever stopped in a bank five minutes to talk with the clerks; when I have received my change I go away and attend to other matters. That is how I like to pray; but there is a way of praying that seems like lounging near the mercy seat as though one had no particular

[27] *Metropolitan Tabernacle Pulpit*, 1871, p 681
[28] *Metropolitan Tabernacle Pulpit*, 1909, p 152
[29] *Metropolitan Tabernacle Pulpit*, 1910, p 99
[30] *Lectures to My Students*, p 63
[31] *Lectures to My Students*, p 71
[32] *Metropolitan Tabernacle Pulpit*, 1910, p 98

reason for being found there.'[33]

It is well known that the Tabernacle congregation spent Monday
nights in prayer: several thousand people gathered for that weekly
meeting. Also the church called for occasional seasons of fasting and
prayer and in some years to a month of special devotion. Spurgeon
also exhorted his brethren in the ministry to spend a day or two with
each other for prolonged times of prayer.[34] But one of his most helpful comments is this: 'I frequently find that I cannot pray as a minister. I find that I cannot sometimes pray as an assured Christian, but
I bless God I can pray as a sinner.'[35]

2.19   Spurgeon the Preacher

Spurgeon's sermons should be returned to throughout one's life and
picked up and read, one a day, for some period, before other things
break that plan. A minister should adopt Spurgeon as his overseer
and pastor. A student fresh out of theological seminary could make
a study of Spurgeon, read the biographies and as many of his 150
books as he can find with a note-book and an index, and thus build
up a full-orbed picture of the man and his ministry. That could not
fail to help anyone to mature as a man of God.

2.19.1   Spurgeon was committed to the divine inspira-
tion of Scripture

'This book is God's hand-writing; these words are God's ... Oh, book
of books! And wast thou written by my God? Then will I bow before
thee. Thou book of vast authority, thou art a proclamation from the
Emperor of Heaven; far be it from me to exercise my reason in con-
tradicting thee ... Oh! if you could ever remember that this Bible was
actually and really written by God ... Oh, tremble, tremble, lest any
of you despise it; mark its authority, for it is the Word of God ... This
is the book untainted by any error; but it is pure unalloyed, perfect
truth. Why? Because God wrote it.'[36] Spurgeon also believed in biblical scholarship and the best translation of the original. 'I would say
that no Baptist should ever fear any honest attempt to produce the

---

[33] *Metropolitan Tabernacle Pulpit*, 1892, pp 206–7
[34] *Lectures to My Students*, p 51
[35] *Metropolitan Tabernacle Pulpit*, 1870, pp 559–60
[36] *New Park Street Pulpit*, 1855, pp 111–2

correct text and an accurate interpretation of the Old and New Testaments. For many years Baptists have insisted upon it that we ought to have the Word of God translated in the best possible manner. All we want is the exact mind of the Spirit, as far as we can get it.'[37]

He preached from every part of Scripture. It was for him the Aeolian harp through which the wind of the Spirit was always sweeping. He was not a man given to speculative theories. 'I do not know what may be the peculiarity of my constitution, but I have always loved safe things. I have not, that I know of, one grain of speculation in my nature.'[38] He knew his God-given commission was to preach the word. 'I have been charged with being a mere echo of the Puritans, but I would rather be the echo of truth than the voice of falsehood.'[39]

2.19.2   Spurgeon preached the gospel of Jesus Christ

He wrote, 'The best, surest, and most permanent way to fill a place of worship is to preach the gospel and to preach it in a natural, simple, interesting, earnest way.'[40] Paul Cook comments, 'Spurgeon's handling of the Scriptures, his exposition of the Word and his preaching were all conditioned, rightly we believe, by the gospel. This probably accounts for the lack of a clear distinction in his preaching between ministry to the saints and gospel preaching to sinners. All his sermons are "gospel sermons". He can visualise no motivation and godly action on the part of believers apart from the gospel and certainly no hope for unbelievers.'[41]

In that gospel, substitution was at its heart. 'It is the very marrow of the whole Bible, the soul of salvation, the essence of the gospel.' Spurgeon once said, 'I feel that if Christ did not actually and literally die as my substitute, the just for the unjust, I am not saved, and never can be at rest in my heart again. I renounce all preaching whatsoever if substitution be not the leading feature of my theme, for there is nothing worthy preaching when that is gone. I regard that doctrine as the fundamental truth of the gospel.'

---

[37] *Metropolitan Tabernacle Pulpit*, 1881, p 343

[38] *The Autobiography*, I, p 193

[39] *An All Round Ministry*, p 17

[40] *Sword and Trowel*, 1883, XIX, p 421

[41] *Foundations*, Spring 1992, 'Where is the God of Spurgeon?' p 5

2.19.3 Spurgeon's sermons were full of the Lord Jesus Christ

'Preach Christ, that is the magnet; he will draw his own to himself. And, dear friends, if we want to see conversions there must be more preaching, more constant preaching of Christ; Christ must be in every sermon, and he must be top and bottom of all the theology that is preached.'[42] In his very first sermon in the new Tabernacle he declared, 'I would propose that the subject of the ministry of this house, as long as this platform shall stand and as long as this house shall be frequented by worshipers, shall be the person of Jesus Christ.'[43]

Spurgeon would often quote the words of Joseph Hart at the conclusion of his hymn, 'Come ye sinners, poor and needy' which say 'None but Jesus, None but Jesus, Can do helpless sinners good.' After he had been a preacher for fifteen years he could say, 'I have been preaching nothing but this name and it has a savour about it sweeter than ever; and if I had but one word more to speak, methinks this should be it: none but Jesus, none but Jesus.'[44] Paul Cook comments, 'As far as Spurgeon was concerned the eternal decrees, the OT revelation, the incarnation and even the resurrection, ascension, Pentecost and the growth of the church all hinged upon Jesus Christ and him crucified.'[45]

2.19.4 Spurgeon applied the Word of God plainly and passionately

He deplored the cultivation of oratorical rhetoric that had spread throughout the Victorian pulpit. 'Oh, that all would tell the gospel out in plain words! I long that all may understand what I have to say: I would be more simple if I knew how. The way of salvation is far too important a matter to be the theme of oratorical displays. The cross is far too sacred to be made a pole on which to hoist the flags of our fine language.'[46]

He poured his whole self into his sermons. 'I remember, when I have preached at different times in the country, and sometimes here, that my whole soul has agonized over men, every nerve of my body

---

[42] *Metropolitan Tabernacle Pulpit*, 1874, p 94

[43] *Metropolitan Tabernacle Pulpit*, 1861 p 169

[44] *Metropolitan Tabernacle Pulpit*, 1864, p 484

[45] *Foundations, ibid*

[46] *Metropolitan Tabernacle Pulpit*, 1886, p 28

has been strained and I could have wept my very being out of my eyes and carried my whole frame away in a flood of tears, if I could but win souls.'[47] He confessed to wishing to leave the confines of the pulpit and to come among the people of the congregation to speak to them personally: 'I feel that I want to go down these stairs, and round these galleries, and to pick out men and women who are being tempted not to pray again, and to give each of them a brotherly grip of the hand, and to say, "Do not cease to plead for thy life; do not cease to look to Jesus on the tree. Hope thou in him; it is Satan's desire to ruin thee by leading thee to despair." '[48]

2.20   Pulpit Preparation and Notes

Spurgeon prepared his Sunday sermon on Saturday evening, a period which could not be disturbed. In mid-October, 1882, the Prime Minister, W E Gladstone, invited Spurgeon to number 10, Downing Street for dinner on the following Saturday night. Spurgeon replied briefly, 'October 24, 1882. I cannot be out on a Saturday night for it is the only time I have to get my sermons.'[49] Visitors would be welcome to his home throughout the day, and then at 6 p.m. he would smile and say, "Now my friends, I must bid you 'Good-bye' and turn you out of this study. You know what a number of chickens I have to scratch for and I want to give them a good meal tomorrow."[50]

When a number of ministers asked him what methods he used to find his sermons he replied, 'All through the week I am on the look-out for material that I can use on the Sabbath; but the actual work of arranging it is left until Saturday evening, for every other moment is fully occupied in the Lord's service. I have often said that my greatest difficulty is to fix my mind upon the particular texts which are to be the subjects of discourse on the following day. As soon as any passage of Scripture really grips my heart and soul, I concentrate my whole attention upon it, look at the precise meaning of the original, closely examine the context so as to see the special aspect of the text in its surroundings and roughly jot down all the thoughts that occur to me concerning the subject, leaving to a later period the or-

---

[47] *Metropolitan Tabernacle Pulpit*, 1898, p 55
[48] *Metropolitan Tabernacle Pulpit*, 1895, p 475
[49] British Museum, *Gladstone Papers*, Vol CCCXCII, No 44477, f 150
[50] *The Full Harvest*, p 310

derly marshalling of them for presentation to my hearers.'[51] Then his wife might join him in the study and read to him, from a pile of commentaries which he had brought down from the shelves, the opinions of those authors on the Sunday text, and gradually the best outline would become clear. Spurgeon would leave to the Sunday afternoon, the final arrangement of divisions, sub-divisions and illustration for the evening sermon.

Spurgeon took into the pulpit a brief outline from which he spoke extemporaneously. He rejected the method of memorising a sermon as 'a wearisome exercise of an inferior power of the mind and an indolent neglect of other and superior faculties.'[52] He also rejected the reading of a manuscript saying, 'The best reading I have ever heard, tasted of paper, and has stuck in my throat. I have not relished it, for my digestion is not good enough to dissolve foolscap.'[53]

The sermon outlines were a well-organised organic unity, and he needed nothing else. Horton Davies writes of their 'orderly sequence and their headings, each of which was the summary of a lesson.'[54] Spurgeon had gained this approach from his Puritan mentors and the freedom it gave him in the pulpit was a reason his audience found it easy to follow him and to remember what he said. But Spurgeon had added to Puritan theology (which addressed men's affections) a zealous directness which characterised the early Methodists and the later Primitive Methodists: 'Seek the fire of Wesley, and the fuel of Whitefield,' he told his students.[55]

2.21 The Metropolitan Tabernacle Pulpit

In 1855, in the second year of his London ministry, Spurgeon began to publish weekly sermons. They were issued continuously until 1917 when a shortage of paper brought their production to a halt. When the first issues of *The New Park Street Pulpit* appeared in 1855, it was considered a trial venture, another supplement to the 'penny pulpits' to which Spurgeon had already contributed an occasional sermon. He did not expect to publish a regular series, but the initial demand for his sermons was so great that the weekly issues were continued

---

[51] *The Full Harvest*, pp 311–2

[52] *Lectures to My Students*, p 153

[53] Quoted by Thielicke, *Encounter with Spurgeon*, p 238

[54] *Worship and Theology in England from Newman to Martineau, 1850–1900*, p 338

[55] *Lectures to My Students*, p 83

through the year, and then became a regular series.

The first five volumes of the series, *The New Park Street Pulpit*, were composed of single sermons of eight pages of small type, which sold individually for a penny. At the end of the year, the single sermons were gathered together and the approximately fifty-two issues published as a single volume. In 1963 this set of six volumes was reprinted by the Banner of Truth as facsimiles of the originals at 75 pence a copy. In the late 1970's Pilgrim Publications of Pasadena, Texas, reprinted them in 3 double volumes. The seventh volume in this series of Spurgeon's sermons was the first under the new title of *The Metropolitan Tabernacle Pulpit.* It was the only volume to have been printed in that same small typeface. The following year, 1863, the duty on paper was abolished which allowed Passmore & Alabaster, the publishers, to expand the eight pages of small type to twelve pages of larger, more readable type. When Pilgrim Publications undertook the heroic task of reprinting all 63 volumes (which they completed in 1980) their first volume had to be carefully introduced to the American market, 'only this first volume has the smaller type.'

When they first appeared some booksellers were cool to the idea of a weekly sermon. In the university town of Cambridge the bookshops refused to sell them and they had to be purchased from a green-grocer. Spurgeon's advertising promoting the sermons was also a stumbling block to some, but as his quality, staying power and consistency were manifest those criticisms were muted, the demand for the sermons never wavered and the hostility of the booksellers faded. When Passmore and Alabaster took offices in Paternoster Row the respectability of the enterprise was evident to all.

Spurgeon's weekly sermons had a normal circulation of 25,000, although that figure was frequently higher, especially upon the occasion of certain topical sermons such as the Mutiny, or the death of the Prince Consort. His best-selling single sermon was on 'Baptismal Regeneration' and sold 350,000 copies when printed as a pamphlet. By 1863, when the 500th weekly issue appeared, his sermons had already sold more than 8 million copies. At the time of his death 50 million copies had been sold. By today the figure has reached over 300 million copies.

The first language into which Spurgeon's sermons were published in translation was Welsh. Forty more languages were to follow. Over the years Spurgeon collected amazing evidence of their international influence. When David Livingstone went to Africa he carried some with him. His daughter discovered a copy of one of them in one of his cases. It was well-thumbed with a penciled comment, 'very good, D L.' A commander of a garrison in India recalled to Spurgeon that his troops had gathered under the trees each Sunday to hear one of his sermons read aloud. The sermon, 'Compel them to Come in,' preached in the New Park Street church on December 5th 1858 by the 24 year-old Spurgeon, when published in the New Park Street Pulpit of 1859 (p16) was responsible for the conversion of 300 people. But 1859 was a remarkable year in the history of the Christian Church.

One man, anxious to spread these sermons, purchased 250,000 copies, had them specially bound 'in the best style' and then sent copies to every crowned head in Europe, every member of parliament, every student in every university in Britain, and all the principal householders in Ireland. It was claimed that his sermons could be found in two-thirds of the homes of Ulster. There were places, it is said, where people failed to recognise the names of Gladstone or Disraeli, but responded at once to 'Spurgeon'.[56] A Scotsman expressed the wish that some day before he died he would like to go to London 'to see Madame Tussaud's and hear Mr. Spurgeon'.[57]

Ian MacLaren (Dr John Watson) described the way in which issues of Spurgeon's sermons were awaited by the people of his Scottish village. He could remember when his employer went to town his wife called after him, "and John, dinna forget Spurgeon." Once a week the family would gather together and one would read the sermon: 'it seemed to me good reading — slow, well-pronounced, reverent, charged with tenderness and pathos. No one slept or moved, and the firelight falling on the serious faces of the stalwart men, and the shining of the lamps on the good grey heads, as the gospel came, sentence by sentence, to every heart, is a sacred memory, and I count that Mr Spurgeon would have been mightily pleased to have been in such meetings of homely folk.'[58]

When Spurgeon visited an area the congregation consisted of people familiar with his sermons through reading the Metropolitan Tabernacle Pulpit. W Y Fullerton told the story of an old man who lived in a country district which was to be visited by Spurgeon. He inquired of his employer if he might attend Spurgeon's afternoon service and was told that he could go only if he had finished the entire

[56]*Sword and Trowel*, XVIII, 1882, p 502

[57]*Contemporary Review*, LXI, March 1892, p 302

[58]Ian MacLaren [Dr John Watson], "Dinna Forget Spurgeon," in *His Majesty Baby and Some Common People*, London, 1902, p 163

day's work. The old man was up before dawn working in the fields, and with every sweep of his scythe he was heard to chant, "Spurgeon! Spurgeon! Spurgeon!" until he had completed the day's work and was off to attend the services.[59]

In the USA there was an immediate large audience for his sermons. American preachers such as Finney, Nettleton, Moorhouse, and Moody came to Britain to preach. Spurgeon was often urged to go to the USA but refused. The Boston Redpath Lyceum Bureau tried for years to get him on the American circuit, guaranteeing all of his expenses plus 1,000 dollars in gold for every lecture delivered, but even that failed to tempt him across the Atlantic. Yale invited him to deliver one of Lyman Beecher series of lectures on preaching, but in vain. American evangelists campaigned across Britain, and some Englishmen preached in the USA, but Spurgeon sent his sermons and stayed in the Tabernacle. He told Dale, 'I sit on my own gate, and whistle my own tunes, and am quite content'.[60]

The first volume of his sermons sold 20,000 in America. Dr Joseph Cook of Boston could reminisce on the occasion of Spurgeon's death of his teenage years when he was a boarder at the Philips Exeter Academy in 1854 and a solitary Christian in the school. On the Lord's Day he would climb upstairs to an empty classroom and read aloud a sermon by this young English preacher then barely known in the USA. The popularity of his sermons brought Americans to the Metropolitan Tabernacle in droves. The Boston Watchman reported that 'during the tourist season, more of the states of America are seated in his congregation than in any congregation in the United States.'[61] 'Our first question to returning friends,' wrote a reporter for the *North American Review*, 'is "Did you see the Queen?" and then, "Did you hear Spurgeon?"'[62] After U S President Garfield died, his wife Lucretia, was clearing up his papers in the White House and she discovered a folded programme of a Tabernacle service. Lucretia Garfield wrote to Spurgeon to inform him that her grief was lessened by the memory of the inspiration she and her husband had received attending one of his services.[63] For the amusement of the American tourists as the Sunday buses would roll over the bridge to

[59]Fullerton, *C H Spurgeon, a Biography*, London, 1920, p 125

[60]A W W Dale, *Life of R W Dale*, London, 1898, p 339

[61]*The Watchman*, November 24, 1881

[62]*North American Review*, 86, [1858], 275

[63]Ms letter from Lucretia Garfield, August 29, 1882, in Spurgeon Papers, Spurgeon's College

the south side of the Thames, conductors would shout out, "Over the water to Charlie!"

The Metropolitan Tabernacle Pulpit covered all America, but a decline in their sales came after his hatred to the institution of slavery was publicised there. Spurgeon had invited a fugitive slave, John Andrew Jackson, to address the New Park Street congregation in the early years of his ministry. His outspoken anti-slavery remarks were pared from the text of the American edition of his sermons in order that they might not offend a portion of his American readers. When Henry Ward Beecher wrote to Spurgeon and protested that this had been done Spurgeon replied, 'I believe slavery to be a crime of crimes, a soul destroying sin, and an iniquity which cries aloud for vengeance.'[64] He then had a letter published in the *Watchman and Reflector* which was widely reprinted in American journals, declaring, 'I do from my inmost soul detest slavery anywhere and everywhere, and though I commune at the Lord's Table with men of all creeds, yet with a slave-holder I hold no fellowship of any kind or sort.[65] Spurgeon's pronouncements resulted in a large crowd gathering in front of a Virginian courthouse for the ceremonial burning of Spurgeon's sermons.[66] From 1860 until the post-war years, the sale of Spurgeon's sermons in the USA was negligible. Yet American Christians from the north never lost their love for him nor their appetite for the *Metropolitan Tabernacle Pulpit.* 'Everything that I could get hold of in print that he ever read, I read,' testified D L Moody, who crossed the Atlantic in 1867 to see him. 'My eyes just feasted upon him, and my heart's desire for years was accomplished.'

2.22 Spurgeon's Letters

No section on the literary labours of Spurgeon would be complete without a post-script on his letters. Many people still have copies of his letters handed down to them by parents or grand-parents. That is not surprising since Spurgeon claims 'a weekly average of 500 letters had to be answered.'[67] It would not be possible for him to handle that many and he must have relied upon his secretaries to a great extent. Nevertheless, Spurgeon was certainly a prolific correspondent.

---

[64] J C Carlisle, *C H Spurgeon, An Interpretive Biography,* 1933, p 166

[65] *Op cit,* p 161

[66] *The Times,* July 23, 1860

[67] *The Full Harvest,* p 192

From his early ministry, letters were pouring forth, page after page of rounded legible hand-writing in violet ink, even when arthritis made the holding of the fountain-pen painful. Doubtless he was helped by the excellence of the early postal system, far superior to today's, which made it possible to write to the same person in a single day by three separate posts, and receive an answer to the first letter by the last post that evening. But even so his discipline in correspondence is impressive. 'I am immersed to the chin in letters,' he wrote to his friend William Williams in 1885. His son Charles records; 'He often said, "I am only a poor clerk, driving the pen hour after hour; here is another whole morning gone, and nothing done but letters! letters! letters!"' One of Spurgeon's elders alone preserved some eighty letters from him. The knowledge that he was visiting a certain area would bring a pile of letters inviting him to speak in venues on the way there: 'How many pence we have been fined in the form of postage for replies to these insanely kind demands we will not calculate, but it is rather too absurd!'[68] Spurgeon never handed over the work of replying to letters to secretaries and anything of importance was answered promptly and personally. There is a large collection of his letters in Spurgeon's College and the Banner of Truth has published 170 of the best of them (just about two days' of his letter-writing!) in the 220-page *Letters of Spurgeon* with a brief introduction by Iain Murray.

2.23   Spurgeon's Calvinism

At Waterbeach Spurgeon had been criticised for being 'too Methodistical,' and 'preaching too many invitation sermons,' and he came to the conclusion that many at New Park Street had been influenced by the kind of Baptist theology which was represented in *The Earthern Vessel*, edited by James Wells of the Surrey Tabernacle. This included a pervasive denial of the free offer of the gospel and the need of beseeching men and women to come to Christ. Spurgeon wrote to his father, 'The London people are rather higher in Calvinism than I am, but I have succeeded in bringing one church to my own views, and will trust, with divine guidance, to do the same for another. I am a Calvinist; I love what is called "glorious Calvinism," but "hyperism"

---

[68] *Sword and Trowel*, August, 1878

is too hot-spiced for my palate.'[69] He often said that John Calvin stood on the shoulders of every other divine and his very great sermon on election from 2 Thessalonians 2:13 & 14, preached in New Park Street Chapel on September 2, 1855 indicates the strength of his Calvinistic convictions. It is the longest sermon in all those early years of his preaching, and is found in the very first volume of the *New Park Street Pulpit*[70] and it has often been reprinted. Spurgeon was most anxious that his congregation be clear on the doctrines of grace. Bringing them to a conviction of this was part of his understanding of his responsibility as a faithful minister of Jesus Christ. He never departed from those convictions throughout his long ministry. That was the theology upon which his evangelistic success drew its strength. The often quoted prayer attributed to him, 'Lord, hasten to bring in all thine elect and then elect some more,' is very curious theology however you approach it. The Arminian is no more able to make head or tail of it than the Calvinist! Dr Patricia Kruppa quotes the phrase in her PhD thesis[71] but can give no reference. It is best considered to be apocryphal. Spurgeon once said that he rarely read any story in print about himself which had a shade of truth in it and he cautioned that 'no man's speeches or lectures should be judged by an ordinary newspaper summary, which in any case is a mere sketch, and in many instances a vile caricature.'[72]

One can appreciate the young Spurgeon's wisdom in preaching so unreservedly on the doctrine of election within the first year of his London pastorate. He wanted to make it transparently clear to his congregation that he stood exactly where his distinguished predecessors Gill and Rippon stood on the doctrines of grace. Then, as there was a tincture of hyper-Calvinism in the church, men affected by it would more readily accede to his offers of Christ to all who would hear him, and also be delivered from their hyperism. He once told one of his deacons that he intended to preach in the open air by the side of a river, and the man said to him, 'I do not like it. It is imitating the Methodists.' Spurgeon replied that 'that was more a recommendation than otherwise, and I was happy to run the risk of being called Methodistical.'[73] So also he could say to his congre-

[69] quoted *Charles Haddon Spurgeon — A Preacher's Progress*, by Patricia S Kruppa, New York, 1982, p 7

[70] *New Park Street Pulpit*, 1855, pp 311–22

[71] P S Kruppa, *Charles Haddon Spurgeon — A Preacher's Progress*,

[72] *Eccentric Preachers*, London, 1879, preface

[73] *Metropolitan Tabernacle Pulpit*, 1870, p 258

gation, 'I love the name of Calvin, but I always regard him as sitting on one side of the room; and I love the name of Wesley, but I regard him as occupying another side place in the assembly".[74] His belief in both human responsibility and also in divine sovereignty, (which on rare occasions he would carelessly describe in homiletical short-hand as the Arminian emphasis and the Calvinistic emphasis), he could better espouse in this way: 'If I see in God's Book two truths which I cannot square with one another, I believe them both. There is a middle term somewhere, though I know not where to find it; and for the present I believe without the explanatory truth. There are the two things, God has said them, and they must be true, and it is mine to believe them.'[75]

In one helpful insight he said this to his congregation, 'I couple with what is called Calvinistic doctrine the other doctrine of free agency and responsibility, which seems to me to be equally true. My God is not a mere omnipotent being, who can rule dead material-ism and compel insensible atoms to do his will; but he can rule free agents, leaving them absolutely free, and yet effecting all his pur-poses with them. God's eternal purposes are accomplished, and yet men remain responsible free agents both in their beginning and in their ending. Do you say that you do not understand how this can be? Neither do I, but I believe it.'[76]

It was his Calvinism that caused offence: 'a most superficial gro-cer's back-parlour view of Calvinistic Christianity,' sniffed the nov-elist George Eliot.[77] Henry Ward Beecher, in a series of lectures on preaching delivered at Yale, compared Spurgeon's Calvinism to a camel's hump — an awkward and unnecessary appendage.[78] Spur-geon responded with a lengthy defense of the utility of the camel's hump. He once said that the highest praise he had ever received had been the words of a critic: 'Here is a man who has not moved one inch forward in all his ministry and at the close of the 19th Century is teaching the theology of the first Century and in Newington Butts is proclaiming the doctrines of Nazareth and Jerusalem current 1,800 years ago.' 'Those words,' Spurgeon declared, 'did please me!'[79]

Spurgeon could present the truths of God's sovereignty in a most

---

[74] *Metropolitan Tabernacle Pulpit*, 1875, p 522
[75] *Metropolitan Tabernacle Pulpit*, 1877, p 441
[76] *Metropolitan Tabernacle Pulpit*, 1883, p 245
[77] *George Eliot's Life*, J W Cross, Vol III, p 122
[78] *Beecher's Lectures on Preaching*, p 102
[79] G H Pike, *Life & Work of C H Spurgeon*, vol 3, p 109

winsome and creative manner: 'On the little balcony outside my study windows, I observed a robin frequently coming, so I took an opportunity, one morning, to put some crumbs there, and I have done the same thing every morning since; and my little feathered friend comes close to the window frame and picks up the crumbs and I do not perceive that he has any difficulty about whether those crumbs were laid there for him, or whether I had an electing love toward him in my heart. There were the crumbs, he wanted them and he picked them up and ate them; and I can tell you that, in doing so, he exactly fulfilled my purposes in putting the crumbs there. I thought that he acted very wisely; and I think that if a poor sinner wants mercy and he sees that there is mercy to be had, he had better not pause to ask, "Did God decree me to have it?", but go and take it, and he will then find that in doing so, he is fulfilling God's decrees.'[80]

Of course Spurgeon saw more to Christianity than the five points of Calvinism, but he saw departure from those points in sober terms: 'I firmly believe the five great doctrines of Calvinism are, in some degree, a summary of the rest; they are distinctive points wherein we differ from those who "have erred from the faith, and pierced themselves through with many sorrows". But there are many more doctrines beside these five; and all are alike precious, and all are alike valuable to the true believer's soul, for he can feed upon them to his heart's content.'[81] Paul Cook has urged the church to be like Spurgeon and, 'emphasise the centralities of the faith. Believers are falling out today over secondary issues and at the same time often failing to assent to and maintain the fundamentals of the faith.'[82] That is true. Of course, Spurgeon would not see the doctrines of election or the perseverance of the saints or man's depravity as a 'secondary issue'. He once said, 'I love so much what I believe to be true, that I would fight for every grain of it; not for the "stones" only, but for the very "dust thereof". I hold that we ought not to say that truth is non-essential; it may be non-essential to salvation, but it is essential for something else. Why, you may as well take one of the jewels out of the Queen's crown, and say it is non-essential, she will be Queen all the same! Will anyone dare to tell God that any doctrine is non-essential?'[83]

---

[80] *Metropolitan Tabernacle Pulpit*, 1919, p 534

[81] *Metropolitan Tabernacle Pulpit*, 1898, p 410

[82] *Foundations*, Spring 1992, p 6

[83] *Metropolitan Tabernacle Pulpit*, 1898, p 308

2.24   Spurgeon's Breadth

Spurgeon was a man of convictions: a Calvinist, a Baptist, an opponent of the concept of an established church, a lover of the great hymns from the history of the church who maintained the New Testament simplicity of non-conformist worship, he also had these convictions concerning the purpose of the miraculous gifts of the Spirit: 'The apostles were men who were selected as witnesses because they had personally seen the Saviour — an office which necessarily dies out, and properly so, because the miraculous power also is withdrawn.'[84] And again, 'Although we may not expect and need not desire the miracles which came with the gift of the Holy Spirit, so far as they were physical, yet we may both desire and expect that which was intended and symbolised by them, and we may reckon to see like spiritual wonders performed among us at this day.'[85] Again, 'Those works of the Holy Spirit which are at this time vouchsafed to the Church of God are every way as valuable as those earlier miraculous gifts which have departed from us. The work of the Holy Spirit, by which men are quickened from their death in sin, is not inferior to the power which made men speak in tongues.'[86] On October 31st 1869 he preached a very relevant sermon for today upon the text, 'This is an evil generation: they seek a sign' (Luke 11:20), which he entitled, 'A Word For Those Who Wait For Signs And Wonders.'[87]

Yet, with these avowed convictions carefully and constantly articulated Spurgeon was no bigot. There was a breadth of Christian charity he possessed which is extraordinary. Modernism was his relentless foe and there could be no quarter given in his opposition to it. In this he stood shoulder to shoulder with General Booth of the Salvation Army whose pronouncements on religious unbelief were almost identical to his own. But the two men were not close. Privately, Spurgeon expressed the opinion that Booth was a fool for 'playing at soldiers', while Booth opposed Spurgeon's smoking tobacco and questioned his fitness to pastor the Tabernacle.[88]

To evangelical Christians he was full of grace and truth. His grandfather and father were Congregationalist preachers: pædobaptism was no barrier to preaching in his pulpit or training his stu-

---

[84] *Metropolitan Tabernacle Pulpit*, 1871, p 178
[85] *Metropolitan Tabernacle Pulpit*, 1881, p 521
[86] *Metropolitan Tabernacle Pulpit*, 1884, p 386
[87] *Metropolitan Tabernacle Pulpit*, 1869, p 601
[88] P S Kruppa, *Charles Haddon Spurgeon — A Preacher's Progress*, p 451

dents for the ministry. The first principal of the Pastor's College, George Rogers, was a Congregationalist. But none of those men could have been members of the Metropolitan Tabernacle. Spurgeon said, 'Surely to be a Baptist is not everything. If I disagree with a man on 99 points, but happen to be one with him in baptism — this can never furnish such ground of unity as I have with another with whom I believe in 99 points, and only happen to differ upon one ordinance.'[89] During the Downgrade Controversy it was the evangelical Anglicans who supported him, understanding the issues for which he was being vilified by most Baptists. They welcomed him back to speak at packed meetings of the Evangelical Alliance and gave him a tumultuous reception.

Then we may widen his circle of affection yet more: Spurgeon was helpful to D L Moody. In 1875 he preached a special sermon at the Metropolitan Tabernacle entitled 'Beware of Unbelief' and it had this subtitle: 'A Watchword for Messrs Moody and Sankey's Campaign in South London'. In that sermon he said, 'Here are two men who have for months consecrated themselves to the preaching of the gospel with no object in the world but the winning of souls for Christ. They have no design or object to gain but the sole glory of God. They seek conversions, conversions to Christ only; and brethren, if there were a thousand faults in them, who am I or who are you to judge them, to say we will not help them in such a work and with such motives?'[90] Replying to a correspondent in 1882 who inquired whether he still had the same opinions concerning Moody he wrote, 'What I wrote in 1876 I have never seen any reason to alter. Messrs Moody and Sankey are two blessed men of God and if their converts on that occasion vanished it was no fault of theirs, neither would I have had them refrain for an hour — far from it.'[91] Yet Spurgeon could be critical of them, adding, 'The movement in London had comparatively no link with the churches, and fostered a rival spirit, and hence it did not bring a permanent blessing of increase to the churches.'[92]. Spurgeon also criticised some of the changes in evangelism which became popular following Moody's campaigns. He never used a public appeal for would-be converts to come to the front.[93] Spurgeon was secretly amused by Moody's pronunciation. He told a

[89] *Sword and Trowel*, XXIV, 1883, p 83
[90] *Metropolitan Tabernacle Pulpit*, 1875, p 335
[91] *Letters of Spurgeon*, ed. Iain Murray, 1992, p 155
[92] *Ibid*
[93] See *The Forgotten Spurgeon*, Iain H Murray, pp 176ff

friend that Moody was the only man he knew who could reduce the word 'Mesopotamia', to two syllables.

Moody, in turn, grumbled to his associates that he resented Spurgeon's patronising attitude and his attempts to 'take over' his London campaigns. He was irked when Spurgeon urged that his converts be baptised.[94] Yet in Moody's crusade against modernism he became identified as the public figure who had followed in Spurgeon's steps. He too believed in an infallible Bible. When asked if the story of Jonah and the whale was a myth, Moody replied, 'I stand by Jonah,'[95] and that was unequivocal enough for Spurgeon. In a symbolic gesture, Susannah Spurgeon presented Spurgeon's pulpit Bible to D L Moody. 'This Bible has been used by my beloved husband and is now given with unfeigned pleasure to one in whose hands its service will be continued and extended.'[96]

If Billy Graham is the natural successor of D L Moody, then there are many who agree with Paul Cook, 'If Spurgeon could be described as the modern Elijah then Lloyd-Jones was the modern Elisha upon whom his mantle fell.'[97] Yet the relationship between Graham and Lloyd-Jones was not cordial and the issue was initially over Graham's invitation system of evangelism and later over Graham's cooperation with modernist preachers and Roman Catholics.[98] There is no way one can use the graciousness of Spurgeon towards Moody to justify those who today claim the theology of Spurgeon being unconcerned with Billy Graham's cooperative evangelism. Modernism is the great enemy of the Christian faith and every effort made to blur the distinction between liberalism and Christianity hinders the revival of New Testament religion.

Again, let us widen the circle of Spurgeon's graciousness even further. In 1874 he preached a sermon in Manchester on the subject of conversion and in it related his own conversion, how he had looked to Jesus and in that look of trust had known the salvation of God. Bishop Fraser of Manchester was a High Anglican, and warily watching out for Spurgeon's visit and hearing of his testimony, wrote at length to warn all the Anglicans of Manchester of such teaching on immediate conversion and assurance of salvation. The next

---

[94] J C Pollock, *Moody, A Biographical Portrait*, 1963, p 153

[95] *Ibid*, p 496

[96] W R Moody, *The Life of Dwight L Moody*, 1900, p 447

[97] *Foundations*, Spring 1992, 'The God of Spurgeon' p 2

[98] *Cf* D Martyn Lloyd-Jones, *The Fight of Faith*, Iain Murray, 1990, pp 302–42 and 440–2

Sunday morning, July 19, 1874, Spurgeon responded from his pulpit with a sermon entitled 'Is Conversion Necessary?' upon the text,
'Therefore if any man be in Christ, he is a new creature; old things
are passed away; behold, all things are become new.' (2 Corinthians
5:17) This is how he began that sermon:

> A few days ago I was preaching in Lancashire upon
> the putting away of sin by our Lord Jesus Christ, and the
> consequent peace of conscience enjoyed by the believer.
> In the course of that sermon I related to my own conver-
> sion, with a view of showing that the simple act of looking
> to Jesus brought peace to the soul. Now, the diocese of
> Manchester is presided over by a bishop who has a de-
> servedly high place in public esteem for his zeal, indus-
> try, and force of character; and, feeling that he did not
> agree with me, has had very properly taken an opportu-
> nity to warn the working men whom he addressed against
> drawing improper inferences from my story, and he has
> done this in a manner so courteous that I only wish all
> discussions were conducted in the same spirit. The best
> return I can make for his courtesy is to enlarge upon the
> subject, and carefully guard his utterances from injurious
> inferences, even as he has protected mine. The idea of
> controversy is not upon my mind at all, nor have I any
> other feeling towards Bishop Fraser than that which is
> honestly expressed in a hearty prayer that God may bless
> him; but I am thinking of the many who will read his re-
> marks who, I trust, may afterwards read mine: and as the
> point is one of the utmost conceivable importance, and
> deeply concerns the souls of our hearers, it is well that
> neither should be misunderstood, and that by all means
> a truth so vital should be brought into prominence.[99]

Would that all religious controversies were begun in so irenic a
spirit!

It is necessary for us to show the breadth of Spurgeon's graciousness one degree more. Dr Patricia Stallings Kruppa has put us much
in her debt by her published thesis, *Charles Haddon Spurgeon: A
Preacher's Progress.*[100] But she does not share Spurgeon's convic-

---

[99] *Metropolitan Tabernacle Pulpit*, 1874, p 397
[100] Garland Publishing, Inc New York & London, 1982

tions and does not write from warm affection for him, though a grudging admiration does come through before she has completed her work. Dr Kruppa makes him out to be a Protestant bigot. She writes, 'Spurgeon's anti-Catholicism was a vital ingredient in his intellectual and emotional outlook, colouring his attitudes to ecclesiology, politics, and the State Church. He was absolutely incapable of rendering an impartial judgment upon any matter involving Roman Catholicism. For him, as the journalist W T Stead observed, "the fagots of Smithfield always began to smoke and splutter whenever he saw a Catholic voter approach the ballot-box or an Irish parliament looking in the distance".'[101]

Those words are simply not true: Dr Kruppa has a problem of misinformation. In his autobiography Spurgeon writes, 'I am not an outrageous Protestant generally and I rejoice to confess that I feel sure there are some of God's people even in the Romish Church ... In Brussels, I heard a good sermon in a Romish church. The place was crowded with people, many of them standing, though they might have had a seat for a halfpenny or a farthing; and I stood, too; and the good priest — for I believe he is a good man — preached the Lord Jesus with all his might. He spoke of the love of Christ, so that I, a very poor hand at the French language, could fully understand him, and my heart kept beating within me as he told of the beauties of Christ and the preciousness of his blood, and of his power to save the chief of sinners. He did not say, "justification by faith," but he did say "efficacy of the blood," which comes to very much the same thing. He did not tell us we were saved by grace, and not by our works; but he did say that all the works of men were less than nothing when brought into competition with the blood of Christ, and that the blood of Christ alone could save.

'True, there were objectionable sentences, as naturally there must be in a discourse delivered under such circumstances; but I could have gone to the preacher, and said to him, "Brother, you have spoken the truth;" and if I had been handling his text, I must have treated it in the same way as he did, if I could have done as well. I was pleased to find my own opinion verified, in his case, that there are, even in the apostate church, some who cleave unto the Lord — some sparks of heavenly fire that flicker amidst the rubbish of old superstition, some lights that are not blown out, even by the strong wind of Popery.'[102]

[101] *Review of Reviews*, V March, 1892, p 180 (*Op cit*), p 21
[102] *The Full Harvest*, pp 21–2

Later on that journey he left Chamonix and crossed the mountain pass of the Simplon, and there at the top discovered a hospice run by some monks who invited him and his friends in. 'It pleased me to find that they were Augustinian monks because, next to Calvin, I love Augustine. I feel that Augustine's works were the great mine out of which Calvin dug his mental wealth; and the Augustinian monks, in their acts of charity, seemed to say, "Our master was a teacher of grace, and we will practise it, and give to all comers whatsoever they shall need without money and without price." ... I pray God to bless the good works of these monks of the Augustinian order, and may you and I carry out the spirit of Augustine, which is the true spirit of Christ.'[103]

James Durham of Scotland, one of Spurgeon's Scottish Puritan mentors ('Durham is a prince among spiritual expositors'), wrote a book entitled *The Scandal of Division among the Godly*. And that theme was crucially important to Spurgeon. He entered upon controversy with his brethren as reluctantly as any activity. To preach the gospel of grace in his pulpit and pastor his people was his sole concern, and yet providence constrained him to speak up when the lambs in that congregation were being led astray. Spurgeon said, 'Far be it for me to imagine that Zion contains none but Calvinistic Christians within her walls, or that there are none saved who do not hold our views.' Iain Murray comments, 'In other words Spurgeon saw — what we need to see — that a distinction must be drawn between errors and persons. All that are within the circle of Christ's love must be within the circle of our love, and to contend for doctrine in a manner which ignores this truth is a rending of the unity of that Church which is His Body.'[104]

2.25 Spurgeon's Industry

There is a bracing chapter in *The Full Harvest* entitled, 'A Typical Week's Work' (pp309–30) which incidentally illustrates what the church is to pray for when she asks the Lord of the harvest to send forth labourers into the harvest field. We have seen that Saturday night was spent in sermon preparation. Sunday morning he would arrive early at the Tabernacle, choose the hymns for the services and arrange with the precentor what tunes to sing to them. Then there

---

[103] *Ibid*, p 32
[104] *The Forgotten Spurgeon*, 1966, p 73

would be a time of prayer with his officers. After the service he would spend the afternoon in the house of some friends nearby, his own home, 'Westwood', being too far away.

Monday was spent revising the previous day's morning sermon for publication the following Thursday. His secretary would be opening his mail and putting aside the letters which demanded an immediate response. These would be answered in the afternoon. There would often be an elders' meeting in the Tabernacle at 5:30 which then developed into the reception of new members. At 7 p.m. would be the Prayer Meeting, the congregation filling the downstairs and the first gallery of the church. These meetings were constantly varied: missionaries would speak: Spurgeon would always give a message: the meeting ended at 8:30 p.m. promptly. Afterwards Spurgeon would interview members, or prospective members and not infrequently would speak in another church on his way home.

Tuesday morning would be used in completing the work of the sermon before getting to the Tabernacle by 3 p.m. to interview new members. The elders would already have spoken to them and filled in cards with which they were to introduce themselves to Spurgeon. If he was happy with their testimony he would assign an elder or deacon to be their visitor and make arrangements about their baptism. He would see on average 30 people at this time. Tuesday evening he would chair one of the regular meetings of one of the Tabernacle societies and listen with interest to their young leaders, watching to find there prospective students for the Pastors' College. Or there could be a special missionary meeting that night at which he would speak.

Wednesday he would like to keep as a day of rest. That would be a constant battle, but occasionally he managed to take a long drive into the country. He would often visit the Bishop of Rochester in Selsdon Park on those occasions. Thursday morning was principally devoted to letter-writing and literary work in general which he would like to do in the summer house in the garden. Thursday evenings he preached at a crowded Tabernacle. Many ministers from all over London would attend that service and if they had problems would wait to see him afterwards, so that he was frequently home at a late hour.

Friday morning he would prepare his lecture for the college students. That regular afternoon class from 3 p.m. to 5 p.m. with their President was the most important meeting of the week for those young men. For another hour he would talk privately with them and occasionally the College would celebrate the Lord's Supper together. (Spurgeon led the training of over 900 men for the ministry, and arranged their settlement in charges or worked to have new chapels built. Students boarded in twos and threes in the homes of members of the Tabernacle. The church paid their landladies for their board. This was done to remove the levity resulting from many men living together, and to keep them in touch with the people they would be ministering to when their college days were over.) Then on Friday evenings he would often preach in London or he would visit a sick member. He did not often take funeral or wedding services.

Saturday mornings he and his private secretary tried to clear off any arrears of work that had accumulated during the week and that was of enormous variety such as preparing articles for the *Sword and Trowel*, reviewing books, arranging to meet men who were seeking admission to the College and settling various financial matters, until the gong sounded announcing dinner. "Well, we have got through a good morning's work, even if there is not much to show for it," he would say.[105] The greater part of the afternoon would be spent in the garden, and friends might call by, but once the end of the afternoon approached Spurgeon would be thinking of the next morning's sermon. All this labour was done in the context of the most indifferent health.

2.26   Spurgeon's Sagacity

Charles Haddon Spurgeon became John Ploughman, his wise spokesman, that shrewd Englishman full of common sense. For example, he refused to endow the Pastor's College, arguing in a wholly characteristic way, 'Why should I gather money which would remain after I am gone to uphold teachings which I might entirely disapprove? No! Let each generation provide for its own wants.'[106] That is precisely what happened: 'Spurgeon's College remained a strong influence for the Reformed faith until Dr Percy Evans became Principal in 1925. His review of B B Warfield's *The Inspiration and the Authority of the Bible* reveals how far he had departed from an evangelical position.'[107]

---

[105] *The Full Harvest*, p 330
[106] *Pall Mall Gazette*, XXXIX, June 19, 1884, p 11
[107] Paul Cook, 'The God of Spurgeon,' *Foundations*, 1992, p 4

Spurgeon's involvement in the College was comprehensive, even to arbitrating in affairs of the heart. He came to hear that one of the students had got engaged to two girls at the same time. So he invited them both to the College. Then he sent for the student, and, confronting him with both women, made him make a choice of one. In Carlisle's biography the story is told with two young women, while William Williams in his memories of Spurgeon has the President parading three girls before the startled student. The former is probably the correct version. The story has Solomonic overtones.

In an age when ministers were not maintained by their churches as they should have been, Spurgeon used his authority to encourage a more responsible spirit. The *Metropolitan Tabernacle Pulpit* related this incident in Spurgeon's life: 'I remember mentioning one day to a man who had considerable property that his poor minister had a large family and could scarcely keep a coat on his back. I said I wondered how some Christian men who profited under the ministry of such a man did not supply his needs. He answered that he thought it was a good thing for ministers to be poor, because they could sympathise with the poor. I said, "Yes, yes, but then, don't you see, there ought to be one or two that are not poor to sympathise with those who are rich." I would give them the opportunity, certainly, and let the poor pastor now and then have the power to sympathise with both classes. He did not seem to see my argument, but I think there is a good deal in it.'[108]

Yet with all his shrewdness Spurgeon was an open, guileless man. He told a would-be biographer, "You may write my life across the sky; I have nothing to conceal."[109] The epithets, 'child-like' and 'trusting' appear over and over in the descriptions of those who knew him. Lord Shaftesbury wrote that he had, 'the openness and simplicity of a child': W T Stead wrote, 'He looked upon the world with a child-like eye': Newman Hall said, 'That which often impressed me was his child-likeness': R W Dale said, 'The strength of the man is blended with the gentleness of a spirit wonderfully child-like.' The Metropolitan Police once discovered a professional beggar's handbook listing the names of potential donors. The list of those counted easy targets for charity was labeled the 'Soft Tommies' and heading the list was the name, 'C H Spurgeon.'[110]

---

[108] *Metropolitan Tabernacle Pulpit*, 1880, p 552
[109] *Charles Haddon Spurgeon, Personal Reminiscences*, William Williams, p 13
[110] James Ellis, *Spurgeon Anecdotes*, London, 1892, p 142

2.27 The End

At a time when there was much emphasis upon the rapture of the saints at the coming of Christ Spurgeon was unenthusiastic: 'If I die not I shall have lost what thousands have had who died, namely, actual fellowship with Christ in the grave. Let me have it, let me have it. Let me wear the clay-cold shape of death that was once Christ's, and sleep within the sepulchre as Christ did. To die and rise again, and be with Him for ever is to complete the circle of the perfect.'[111]

That desire was granted to Spurgeon when the end came to this memorable life on January 31st 1892. Towards midnight he whispered to his secretary, J W Harrald, "Remember, a plain stone. 'C H S' and no more. No fuss."

Three days later *The Times* published an obituary written by Dr Joseph Parker: 'Mr Spurgeon was absolutely destitute of intellectual benevolence. If men saw as he did they were orthodox; if they saw things in some other way they were heterodox, pestilent and unfit to lead the minds of students or inquirers. Mr Spurgeon's was a superlative egotism; not the shilly-shallying, timid, half-disguised egotism that cuts off its own head, but the full-grown, over-powering, sublime egotism that takes the chief seat as if by right. The only colours which Mr. Spurgeon recognised were black and white.'[112] But that was not the last word on Spurgeon's life as the international celebrations of affection and the re-publication of virtually everything he wrote 100 years later have proved. Perhaps today he is having more influence in the world than he was 100 years ago. God will honour the life and ministry of Charles Haddon Spurgeon who loved his Saviour, until that Lord Jesus Christ comes again.

---

[111] *Metropolitan Tabernacle Pulpit*, 1868, p 599
[112] *The Times*, February 3, 1892

Chapter 3

Spurgeon and his Gospel Invitations

Two subjects are antecedent to an appreciation of the glorious and uninhibited way in which Spurgeon addressed unbelievers with the free invitations of the gospel. The first is the historical setting, he was primarily an evangelist preaching during a time of spiritual awakening. The second is his Puritan theology.

3.1 The historical setting — an evangelist in a time of awakening

Few students of the life of C H Spurgeon seem to have realised that his ministry commencing at New Park Street in 1855 was a harbinger of the great prayer revival of 1858. That notable revival which swept across America and Britain was called 'the prayer revival' because multiplying numbers gathering for prayer meetings was the way in which the mighty power of the Holy Spirit came to revive and multiply the Church. Every revival has its own divine character. The prayer revival had the stamp of Zechariah 12:10 etched upon it: 'And I will pour upon the house of David and of Jerusalem's inhabitants a spirit of grace and supplication, they will look on me, the one they pierced and they will mourn for him as one mourns for an only child.'
A powerful visitation of the Holy Spirit had already attended

the boy preacher's ministry in the village of Waterbeach.[1] He first preached at New Park Street church on the South Bank of the Thames in December 1853. He became the minister there during 1854. For those days the congregation was small, about 200. By the autumn of that same year 1854, 500 were in regular attendance at the weekly prayer meeting.[2] The character of those prayer meetings is described by Spurgeon himself:

> 'When I came to New Park Street Chapel, it was but a mere handful of people to whom I first preached; yet I can never forget how earnestly they prayed. Sometimes, they seemed to plead as if they could really see the Angel of the Covenant present with them, and as if they must have a blessing from him. More than once, we were all so awe-struck with the solemnity of the meeting, that we sat silent for some moments while the Lord's power appeared to overshadow us; and all I could do on such occasions was to pronounce the benediction, and say, "Dear friends, we have had the Spirit of God here very manifestly to-night; let us go home and take care not to lose his gracious influences." Then came down the blessing; the house was filled with hearers, and many souls were saved. I always give all the glory to God, but I do not forget that he gave me the privilege of ministering from the first to a praying people. We had prayer-meetings in New Park Street that moved our very souls. Every man seemed like a crusader besieging the New Jerusalem, each one appeared determined to storm the Celestial City by the might of intercession; and soon the blessing came upon us in such abundance that we had not room to receive it.'[3]

It is important to understand that Spurgeon was ministering in a time of spiritual awakening. Every service was a great evangelistic occasion. Converts were interviewed every Tuesday afternoon, the whole afternoon being devoted to that exercise in which CHS was assisted by his helpers. We can appreciate therefore the manner

---

[1] Arnold Dallimore has an excellent chapter describing the boy preacher at Waterbeach. *Spurgeon — A New Biography*, Banner of Truth, 1985

[2] Iain Murray, *The Forgotten Spurgeon*, p 33 Banner of Truth, 1966

[3] *The Autobiography*, vol 1, p 361

in which Spurgeon sought to persuade the uncommitted to believe in Christ for salvation. In exposition he would often tell his hearers how to be saved and then urge them to be saved. The fact that he was a reaper of souls explains too the fact that he did not follow the Puritans in using the systematic method of consecutive textual preaching. For him it was imperative that he be gripped or bitten by a text or theme. He often agonised to get his subject or text but once he arrived at that his method was to be expository in opening it up with an arresting introduction an expository content and a persuasive conclusion aimed at the heart and conscience. His preaching was doctrinally clear and as we shall see he was totally uninhibited in inviting and urging sinners to close with the free offers of the gospel.

As we have seen, the work at New Park Street began to increase from the time of Spurgeon's arrival early in 1854. In the 37 years of his ministry 14,000 members joined the church, over 900 had been trained in the college, and over 300 million copies of his books and sermons had been sold.

I have suggested that Spurgeon was a harbinger of the prayer revival of the 1858 onwards. During a sermon preached in March 1858 he described his joy at hearing of the revival in America.

> 'My soul has been made exceedingly full of happiness by the tidings of a great revival of religion throughout the United States. Some hundred years, or more ago, it pleased the Lord to send one of the most marvellous religious awakenings that was ever known ; the whole of the United States seemed shaken from end to end with enthusiasm for hearing the Word of God; and now after the lapse of a century, the like has happened again. The monetary pressure has at length departed, but it has left behind it the wreck of many mighty fortunes. Many men, who were once princes, have now become beggars, and in America, more than in England, men have learned the instability of all human things. The minds of men, thus weaned from the earth by terrible and unexpected panic, seem prepared to receive tidings from a better land, and to turn their exertions in a heavenly direction. You will be told by any one who is conversant with the present state of America, that wherever you go there are signs that religion is progressing with majestic strides. The great revival, as it is now called, has become the com-

mon market talk of merchants. It is the theme of every newspaper; even the secular press remark it, for it has become so astonishing that all ranks and classes of men seem to have been affected by it. Apparently without any cause whatever, fear has taken hold of the hearts of men; a thrill seems to be shot through every breast at once; and it is affirmed by men of good repute, that there are at this time, towns in New England where you could not, even if you searched, find one solitary, unconverted person. So marvellous — I had almost said, so miraculous — has been the sudden and instantaneous spread of religion throughout the great empire, that it is scarcely possible for us to believe the half of it, even though it should be told us.'[4]

When Spurgeon came to London the congregation increased dramatically. It was necessary to move to Exeter Hall in the Strand which seated 4000 and then to the Music Hall, Royal Surrey Gardens, which accommodated 10,000. From these crowds came a harvest of converts, a harvest which continued to be reaped throughout his ministry. Preaching on December 21st 1862, CHS reported that he had not preached a sermon during that year which had not resulted in conversions.

Did the crowds wane? In 1867 the Tabernacle was in need of redecoration and for four weeks one service each Lord's Day was held at the Agricultural Hall in North London. It was not suited for an auditorium and it was feared that even Spurgeon's wonderful voice would fall far short of reaching the maximum number of about 25,000 that could be packed in through a large sector being made available for standing only. Thousands were turned away. In fact, the preacher was heard in every corner. The emphasis was on repentance and the way of salvation. A secular newspaper described a service at the Metropolitan Tabernacle on Oct 22nd 1876. It was the custom for the three thousand ticket holders to stay at home once a quarter to allow outsiders to attend. By a quarter past six every seat was occupied and the aisles thronged. But the deacons were practised in the art of fitting people into every nook and cranny so that while the tabernacle was built to accommodate 6,000 in fact it was nearer 7,000 that were packed into every available space. The doors being closed,

---

[4] *New Park Street Pulpit*, 1858, p 161

the lecture hall was then used to accommodate the overflow.[5]

In addition to his own church, CHS preached on many occasions at other centres always to large congregations seldom under several thousands and mostly with evangelism in mind. Where did he find the physical energy required to reach such large crowds unaided by modern technology? He answers this himself in a sermon at Exeter hall in January 1860 on Amos 9:13.

> 'We find ourselves able to preach ten or twelve times a week, and we find we are the stronger for it. I meet brethren in the ministry who are able to preach day after day and are not half so fatigued as they were. I met one brother who has been kept every day from 6:00 pm to 2 in the morning. "Oh," said one of the members, "our minister will kill himself". "Not he," said I, "that is the kind of work that will kill no man. It is preaching to sleepy congregations that kills good ministers." So when I saw him his eyes were sparkling and I said to him, "Brother you do not look like a man who is being killed!" "Killed, my brother!" he replied, "why I am living twice as much as I did before, I was never so happy, never so hearty and never so well. I sometimes lack my rest when my people keep me up so late but I should like to die of such a disease as that — the disease of being so greatly blessed!"[6]

Sometimes in the early years he preached in many churches in the interest of encouraging gifts for the building of the Metropolitan Tabernacle. A weekly routine developed. This is described by Geoff Thomas under the heading 'Spurgeon's Industry.'

It is needful to point out that the life and ministry of Spurgeon can be discouraging to those labouring during times of spiritual apathy and indifference. It would be easy to be tempted with the thought that our labour is useless compared to the wondrous, almost fairy story description of the attraction of Spurgeon's preaching. Crowds do not flock to hear us. Holden Pike in his biography tells of one minister who took a pastor to hear Spurgeon. When he came out, this pastor said that if that was what preaching was, then he resolved never ever to preach again! But we must allow for the exceptional and give glory to the Lord for the diversity of gifts that he bestows.

---

[5] Holden Pike, vol 5, p 183ff
[6] *New Park Street Pulpit*, 1860, p 83

It is about once a century that all the gifts seem to combine in one person. Spurgeon had a voice like Pavarotti, rich and powerful, a magnetic personality, a brilliant intellect, an obedient memory, and an amazingly fertile and imaginative mind. Let us give the praise to our Saviour for that. We have to struggle with our limitations. Nevertheless we can make sure that our Calvinistic doctrine inspires and helps our preaching rather than inhibits or hinders it. In that context we turn from the apportioning of Spurgeon's time to his example with regard to doctrine. The spiritual climate may be different but the doctrine governing our gospel invitations does not change.

3.2   Spurgeon's theology — wholehearted proclamation of the doctrines of grace

At the beginning of his ministry in London CHS made the 1689 Confession of Faith the doctrinal standard of the church. That Reformed and Puritan creed represented exactly Spurgeon's doctrinal convictions which he proclaimed clearly and powerfully and from which he never altered course.

Preaching a sermon on the text, 'And you will not come to me that you might have life' (Jn 5:40), with the title *Free Will a Slave*,[7] Spurgeon began as follows, 'Free will is one of the great guns of the Arminians, mounted on the top of their walls, and often discharged with terrible noise upon the poor Christians called Calvinists. I intend to spike this gun this morning!' In this sermon he does justice to both human inability and human responsibility. He humbles his hearers — 'We do not preach this doctrine of inability to excuse you but to humble you. The possession of a bad nature is my fault as well as my terrible calamity.'

That affirmation can easily lead to wrong conclusions. There is a denomination in England known as the Gospel Standard. As is invariably the case, there are outstanding believers to be found within this grouping. The articles of faith to which all have to subscribe are daunting and it is no surprise that the decline of this denomination is well above the average decline that is being experienced by most groupings in England. Incorporated into the Gospel Standard doctrinal basis is the following article:

---

[7] *New Park Street Pulpit*, 1855, p 395

'For ministers in the present day to address unconverted persons, or indiscriminately all in a mixed congregation, calling upon them to savingly repent, believe
and receive Christ, or perform any other acts dependent
upon the new creative power of the Holy Spirit, is, on
the one hand to imply creature power and the on other,
to deny the doctrine of special redemption.'

This statement results from a failure to understand that it is essential to hold firmly to the truth of human responsibility. God
sovereignly commands all men everywhere to repent and believe the
gospel. The fact that man has been crippled by the fall does not excuse him any more than his addiction to alcohol can cancel out the
drunkard's accountability.

The 18th century High Calvinists held that it was necessary for
sinners to have a warrant in order to believe to salvation. For them
it was not right to exhort faith as the duty of those unable to believe.
That was the position those who originated the 'duty faith' articles
stated above. In his day Andrew Fuller turned the tide against hyper-
Calvinism through his book, *The Gospel Worthy of all Acceptation*.
The hyper-Calvinist position was held by Spurgeon's contemporary,
James Wells of the Surrey Tabernacle. He launched an attack on
Spurgeon in the magazine *The Earthen Vessel* in 1857.

Spurgeon addressed this subject in some detail in a sermon
preached in 1863 which carried the title *The Warrant of Faith*, based
on the text, 'And this is his commandment that we should believe on
the name of his Son Jesus Christ' (1 Jn 3:23). What it is that we are
to believe occupied his first point. Then he spent most of his time
on the warrant of all men to believe, namely, the command of God.
He asserts, 'The warrant for a sinner to believe in Christ is not in
himself in any sense or in any manner, but in the fact that he is commanded there and then to believe on Jesus Christ'.[8] In this sermon
CHS criticised some of the Puritans, namely, Alleine, Baxter, Rogers
of Dedham, Shepherd and Thomas Hooker. This criticism was for
the most part a failure on Spurgeon's part to distinguish between the
warrant of faith and the way to faith. Spurgeon himself and all true
gospel preachers point the way to saving faith with exhortations such
as, 'Read your Bible', 'Attend to preaching', 'Mix with Christians',
'Seek the Lord while he may be found, call on him while he is near'.

---

[8] *Metropolitan Tabernacle Pulpit*, 1863, p 531

William Greenhill in a sermon on Ezekiel 18:32, 'What must and can persons do toward their own conversion?' is specific on the practical measures to be taken in the pursuit of faith.[9] After outlining and defining man's natural inability he urges upon them what they ought to do: 'Strive to enter in at the narrow gate, see how corrupt your nature is, look for help from where the command comes.' All this is exhortation to the way of faith. When the Philippian jailer cried out in agony about how he might be saved, Paul did not say that he should go and read Isaiah or attend the next gospel service. He gave him the best answer, 'Believe on the Lord Jesus Christ and you will be saved!' This subject is explored and the difference between the way of faith and the warrant of faith is explained in the magazine *Reformation Today*, issue 122.

That CHS held consistently to the antinomy of divine sovereignty and human responsibility is seen in his clear view of regeneration.

> 'Unless God the Holy Spirit, who works in us to will and to do should operate upon the will and conscience, regeneration is an absolute impossibility, and therefore so is salvation. "What!" says someone, "do you mean to say that God absolutely interposes in the salvation of every man to make him regenerate?" I do indeed!'[10]

In this CHS followed well our Lord, who one moment told Nicodemus of the necessity of new birth from above but the next moment pointed him to faith, 'Whoever believes in him shall not perish but have everlasting life.'

There are ministers who believe the doctrines of grace but never dare to preach them, or if they do their presentation is so obscure that nobody would grasp the nature of the truth. In the sixth chapter of John we have a record of Jesus teaching. Such is the clarity of his sayings, it is impossible to misconstrue what our Lord says. Spurgeon proclaimed the doctrines of grace unambiguously. He despised a general redemption that saves nobody. He preached particular redemption as clearly as you will find it anywhere expressed.

Concerning the doctrine of particular redemption I do not know of any preacher or writer clearer or more aggressive than CHS. This is how he presented that subject:

---

[9]Morning Exercises, Cripplegate, vol 1, p 49

[10]*New Park Street Pulpit*, 1857, p 188

'They believe in an atonement made for everybody; but then, their atonement is just this. They believe that Judas was atoned for just as much as Peter; they believe that the damned in hell were as much an object of Jesus Christ's satisfaction as the saved in heaven; and though they do not say it in proper words, yet they must mean it, for it is a fair inference, that in the case of multitudes, Christ died in vain, for he died for them all, they say; yet so ineffectual was his dying for them, that although he died for them they are damned afterwards. Now, such an atonement I despise — I reject it. I may be called Antinomian or Calvinist for preaching a limited atonement; but I had rather believe a limited atonement that is efficacious for all men for whom it was intended, than an universal atonement that is not efficacious for anybody, except the will of man be joined with it. Why, my brethren, if we were only so far atoned for by the death of Christ that any one of us might afterwards save himself, Christ's atonement were not worth a farthing, for there is no man of us can save himself — no not under the gospel; for if I am to be saved by faith, if that faith is to be my own act, unassisted by the Holy Spirit, I am as unable to save myself by faith as to save myself by good works. And after all, though men call this a limited atonement, it is as effectual as their own fallacious and rotten redemptions can pretend to be. But do you know the limit of it? Christ has bought a "multitude that no man can number." The limit of it is just this: He has died for sinners; whoever in this congregation inwardly and sorrowfully knows himself to be a sinner, Christ died for him; whoever seeks Christ, shall know that Christ died for him; for our sense of need of Christ, and our seeking after Christ, are infallible proofs that Christ died for us. And, mark, here is something substantial. The Arminian says Christ died for him; and then, poor man, he has but small consolation therefrom, for he says, "Ah! Christ died for me; that does not prove much. It only proves I may be saved if I mind what I am after. I may perhaps forget myself; I may run into sin, and I may perish. Christ has done a good deal for me, but not quite enough, unless I do something." But the man who receives the Bible as it is, he says, "Christ died for me, then my eternal life is sure." [11]

Observe how the invitation is woven into the doctrine. Whoever seeks Christ shall know Christ died for him. The doctrine is not permitted to be an obstacle to the sinner but rather turned round to encourage the sinner to come to Christ.

With regard to the doctrine of election Spurgeon refuted those who claim that God elects on the basis of foresight of faith. 'Now God gives faith, therefore he cannot have elected them on account of faith, which he foresaw, — election, we are sure is absolute, and altogether apart from the virtues which the saints have afterwards.' [12]

To Spurgeon, the number of the elect will be very great. He attributed this to the future conversion of the world. 'This world, as I believe, is to be converted to Christ; but not today, nor tomorrow, peradventure not for many an age ... ' [13] Preaching on Psalm 22:27, 21 April, 1872 he used these headings:

1. The conversion of the nations may be expected,

2. This conversion will occur in the usual manner of other conversions, The nations will remember their idolatries against God and the disappointments that have come to them. They will say one to another, "To what purpose have we worshipped these gods of stone?" [what would have Spurgeon have thought of the great stone statues of Marx and Lenin coming down!]

3. The means to accomplish this result are to be found at Calvary. Our text is in a Calvary psalm, its connection is full of sacrificial suffering. If you desire to comprehend its real meaning you must hear it from the dying lips of the incarnate God. It is through the cross that the nations shall fear and tremble and turn to God.' [14]

This point of a wide and generous election is germane to Spurgeon's free invitations of the gospel. It made him fearless. His was no gospel of failure. He was never pessimistic concerning the outcome

[11] *New Park Street Pulpit*, 1858, pp 70–1

[12] *New Park Street Pulpit*, 1855, p 317. The sermon is titled 'Election'

[13] *Metropolitan Tabernacle Pulpit*, 1881, p 327

[14] *Metropolitan Tabernacle Pulpit*, 1872, p 229ff

of the gospel, never in doubt about its victorious outcome. The doctrine of election did not constrict him. He believed that a great number will be gathered and the means of gathering them is by lifting up Christ crucified so that all men might be drawn to him. Corresponding with that was the necessity of freely offering eternal life through union with Christ and inviting all to come freely to him.

He testified to the effectual nature of plain preaching; 'My experience goes to show that there have been persons converted to God by doctrines that some might have thought altogether unlikely to produce that result. I have known the doctrine of the resurrection to bring sinners to Christ; I have heard of scores brought to the Saviour by a discourse upon election — the very sort of people who, as far as I can see, would never have been reached if that truth had not happened to be an angular doctrine that just struck their heart in the right place, and fitted into the crevices of their nature.'[15]

To those who asked whether they were elect CHS said that they could only know that by believing in Christ. 'Do you feel yourself to be a lost guilty sinner? Go straightway to the Cross of Christ, and tell Christ that, and tell him that you have read in the Bible, that "him that comes to him he will in no wise cast out" — look to Christ and believe on him and you shall make proof of your election directly, for so surely as you believe you are elect!'[16]

3.3   The Character of Spurgeon's Gospel Invitations

3.3.1   There was no restriction in his invitations

Holding consistently to the tension of divine sovereignty and human responsibility meant that Spurgeon wholeheartedly and without restriction of any kind, exhorted unconverted persons to repent and believe and to come to Christ as the Son of God and receive him immediately as Lord and Saviour. He addressed all sinners without exception, promising them that if they came to Christ he would in no way cast them out. Not for a moment did he ever think that they could believe and repent by their own power, but he did not allow himself be inhibited by that and nor did he ever encourage confu-

---

[15] *The Full Harvest*, p 241
[16] *New Park Street Pulpit*, 1858, p 406

sion in his listeners. Repent and believe they must to be saved. That
was an immediate and urgent necessity. The details of enablement
were beside the point. He exhorted them to come just as they were
in all their sin and guilt. He guaranteed salvation if they would do
that:

> 'O sinner, you can never perish if you will cast your-
> self at the foot of the cross. If you seek to save yourself
> you shall die. If you come just as you are, all black, all
> filthy, all hell deserving, all ill deserving, I am my Mas-
> ter's hostage, I will be answerable at the day of judgment
> for this matter, if he does not save you.'[17]

Spurgeon never pandered to the idea that gospel invitations
should be confined to the spiritually hungry or those who could trace
some drawing in themselves. For him human responsibility was the
bottom line and he pressed outright responsibility upon all with no
exceptions.

3.3.2   There was flexibility in his invitations

Spurgeon was nothing if he was not flexible. Occasionally there are
sermons which form an appeal or invitation from beginning to end.
An example is the sermon entitled, *Compel them to Come In*, which
was greatly used.[18]

In the short introduction to the 1859 volume of *New Park Street
Pulpit*, Spurgeon testifies that 'scarcely a week occurs without some
case of its usefulness coming to light'. Yet there are sermons which
are purely expository and which do not have any special invitation.
In some sermons he explains the way of salvation but in others not.
His immediate address to the unconverted can be expected at the
beginning of his sermons, in the middle, or at the end, which is mostly
the case, or not at all. It was the general character of the truth and his
evangelistic manner and his persuasiveness and above all, his evident
love for souls that was so wonderfully used.

He used contemporary events in his invitations. At the time of
the total eclipse of the sun he preached a sermon with the title, *The
Solar Eclipse*. The text he chose was; 'I form the light, and create

---

[17] *New Park Street Pulpit*, 1857, p 232
[18] *New Park Street Pulpit*, 1859, p 227

darkness' (Is 45:7). He used this occasion to provide an awesome description of hell:

> 'Soon shall your sun set, and set in everlasting night. A few more months and your gaiety shall be over; your dreams of pleasure shall be dissipated by the terrible wailing of the judgment trump. Can you guess what the Saviour meant when he said, "outer darkness, where there is wailing and gnashing of teeth"? Can any tell except those eclipsed spirits that have these many years been writhing in the torments of eternal judgment: can any tell what is meant by that "outer darkness"? It is darkness so thick that hope which lives anywhere cannot dart even a feeble ray through its impenetrable gloom'.[19]

3.3.3 There was great love in his invitations

Spurgeon had so intense a love for the souls of men that he could declare, 'I remember, when I have preached at different times in the country, and sometimes here, that my whole soul has agonised over men, every nerve of my body has been strained, and I could have wept my very being out of my eyes, and carried my whole frame away in a flood of tears, if I could but win souls. On such occasions, how we preach, as if we had men before us personally, and were clutching them, and begging them to come to Christ! But with all that, I know I never made a soul alive yet, and never shall; and I am perfectly conscious that all the pleadings of all the living ambassadors from God will never induce a sinner to come to Jesus, unless Jesus comes to that sinner'.[20]

Those who heard him testify that they sensed his love for souls. The earnestness of concern which comes through all his sermons evidences the love of Christ for souls. This is a matter sensed rather than documented with words. The issue is perhaps best brought into focus by the way he urged the paramount need of love in his first sermon at New Park Street:

> 'John Bunyan gives a portrait of a man whom God intended to be a guide to Heaven; have you ever noticed how beautiful that portrait is? He has a crown of life

---

[19] *New Park Street Pulpit*, 1858, p 145
[20] *Metropolitan Tabernacle Pulpit*, 1898, p 55

over his head, he has earth beneath his feet, he stands
as if he pleaded with men, and he had the Best of Books
in his hand. Oh! I would that I were, for one moment,
like that pattern preacher; that I could plead with men
as John Bunyan describes. We are all of us ambassadors
for Christ, and we are told that, as ambassadors, we are to
beseech men as though God besought them by us. How
I do love to see a tearful preacher! How I love to see
the man who can weep over sinners; whose soul yearns
over the ungodly, as if he would, by any means and by all
means, bring them to the Lord Jesus Christ! I cannot understand a man who stands up and delivers a discourse
in a cold and indifferent manner, as if he cared not for
the souls of his hearers. I think the true gospel minister will have a real yearning over souls something like
Rachel when she cried, "Give me children, or else I die;"
so will he cry to God, that he may have his elect born, and
brought home to him. And, methinks, every true Christian should be exceedingly earnest in prayer concerning
the souls of the ungodly; and when they are so, how abundantly God blesses them, and how the church prospers!
But, beloved, souls may be damned, yet how few of you
care about them! Sinners may sink into the gulf of perdi-
tion, yet how few tears are shed over them! The whole
world may be swept away by a torrent down the precipice
of woe, yet how few really cry to God on its behalf! How
few men say, "Oh that my head were waters, and mine
eyes a fountain of tears, that I may weep day and night
for the slain of the daughter of my people!" We do not
lament before God the loss of men's souls, as it well becomes Christians to do.'[21]

3.3.4 There was the reality of death and hell in his invitations

Invitational preaching is characterised by earnest pleading, solemn
warning, as well as fervent reasoning, and promises for those who
repent.

Whole sermons such as, *The Smoke of their Torments* as well as

---

[21] *The Autobiography*, vol 1, p 329

descriptions of hell in many sermons were used to reason with his hearers to embrace salvation. Here is an example:

'When the damned jingle the burning irons of their torments, they shall say, "Forever!" When they howl, their cries echo "Forever!"

> *'Forever's written on their racks,*
> *Forever on their chains;*
> *Forever burneth in the fire,*
> *Forever, ever reigns.* '[22]

And again,

'Remember, men may laugh at hell and say there is none; but they must reject their Bibles before they can believe the lie. Men's consciences tell them that,

> *'There is a dreadful hell*
> *And everlasting pains*
> *Where sinners must with devils dwell,*
> *In darkness, fire and chains.* '[23]

In a sermon on death he faces his congregation with that reality by depicting the last moments of the unrepentant sinner:

'And now you feel that you are expiring. Your soul is filled with terror. Black horrors and thick darkness gather round you. Your eye strings break. Your flesh and your heart fail. But there is no kind angel to whisper, "Peace, be still." No convoy of cherubim to bear your soul away straight to yonder worlds of joy. You feel that the dart of death is a poisoned dart; that it has injected hell into your veins; that you have begun to feel the wrath of God before you enter upon that state where you shall feel it to the full.'[24]

3.3.5   There was personal appeal in his invitations

Spurgeon had a way in his preaching of making every person feel that the message was specially for him or her.

On Thursday evening 2 October, 1873, he preached a sermon entitled *Peter's shortest prayer,* "Lord, save me!" In it he urged:

---

[22] *New Park Street Pulpit,* 1855, p124

[23] *New Park Street Pulpit,* 1857, p 79

[24] *New Park Street Pulpit,* 1860, p 148

'I entreat everyone here to pray this personal prayer.
I see some little girls over there; will not each one of you,
my dear children, pray this prayer? — And you working
men who I am so glad to see at this week-night service,
do not go away without presenting your own personal
petitions.'[25]

CHS observed, 'I am so glad to see so large a proportion of men
here. I always have a very great preponderance of men — therefore, I
suppose I am warranted in appealing to you.'[26] It was observed that
sometimes ninety percent of the congregation was male. It is suggested that one reason for this was the pressure of physical crowding
in to the services which was disliked by women.

3.3.6   There was urgency in his invitations

It was Spurgeon's custom to say, 'Remember I have no authority to
ask you to come to Christ tomorrow. The Master has given you no
invitation to come to him next Tuesday. The invitation is "Today if
you will hear his voice, harden not your hearts as in the day of provo-
cation. For the Spirit says today!"'

Concluding one sermon he said, 'For *Now*, mark it, *Now* is the
accepted time to believe on him who justifies the ungodly. Oh! may
the Holy Spirit give you faith that you may be saved now, for then
you will be saved forever!'[27]

Yet Spurgeon disdained using decisionist methods. He fiercely
opposed the slick counselling methods of the enquiry room likening
that to Romish priestcraft. 'Sometimes shut up that enquiry room. I
have my fears about that institution if it be used in permanence, and
as an inevitable part of the services. It may be a very wise thing to invite persons, who are under concern of soul, to come apart from the
rest of the congregation, and have a conversation with godly people;
but if you should ever see that a notion is fashioning itself that there
is something to be got in the private room which is not to be had at
once in the assembly, or that God is more at that penitent form than
elsewhere, aim a blow at that notion at once. We must not come back
by a rapid march to the old way of altars and confessionals, and have
Romish trumpery restored in a coarser form. If we make men think

---

[25] *Metropolitan Tabernacle Pulpit*, 1910, p 103
[26] *New Park Street Pulpit*, 1860, p 484
[27] *New Park Street Pulpit*, 1856, p 240

that conversation with ourselves or with our helpers is essential to
their faith in Christ, we are taking the direct line for priestcraft. In
the gospel, the sinner and the Saviour are come together, with none
between. Speak upon this point very clearly, "You, sinner, sitting
where you are, believing on the Lord Jesus Christ, shall have eternal
life. Do not stop till you pass into an enquiry-room. Do not think it
essential to confer with me. Do not suppose that I have the keys of
the Kingdom of Heaven, or that these godly men and women associ-
ated with me can tell you any other gospel than this, He that believes
on the Son has everlasting life".'[28]

3.3.7 There was the offer of immediate justification in his invitations

Spurgeon was crystal clear in preaching justification by faith and in
denouncing works as a way of righteousness.

'Come to him as you are. But ah, I know that when we sit in our
studies it seems a light thing to preach the gospel and make people
believe in Christ; but when we come to practice it is the hardest thing
in the world. If I were to tell you to do some great thing you would
do it, but simply when it is "Believe, wash and be clean!" you will
not do it. If I said, "Give me ten thousand pounds," you would give
it. You would crawl a thousand miles on your hands and knees, or
drink the bitterest draught that ever was concocted, but this trusting
in Christ is too hard for your proud spirit'.[29]

'When a sinner believes in Christ, his sins positively cease to be,
and what is more wonderful they all cease to be, as Kent says in those
well known lines:

> *Here's pardon for transgressions past,*
> *It matters not how black their cast,*
> *And O, my soul, with wonder view,*
> *For sins to come here's pardon too.*

They are all swept away in one solitary instant; the crimes of
many years; extortions, adulteries, or even murder, wiped away in
an instant.'[30]

---

[28] *An All-Round Ministry*, p 372ff
[29] *New Park Street Pulpit*, 1860, p 64
[30] *New Park Street Pulpit*, 1858, p 415

3.3.8 There was urgent persuasiveness in his invitations

Every valid argument was used in his fervent persuasiveness:

> 'I beseech you, my hearers, by the death of Christ —
> by his agony and bloody sweat — by his cross and passion
> — by all that is holy — by all that is sacred in heaven and
> earth — by all that is solemn in time or eternity — by
> all that is horrible in hell, or glorious in heaven — by
> that awful thought "for ever" — I beseech you, lay these
> things to heart, and remember that if you are damned, it
> will be unbelief that damns you. If you are lost it will be
> because you did not believe in Christ, and if you perish,
> this shall be the bitterest drop of gall — that you did not
> trust the Saviour.'[31]

Preaching during 1881 from Revelation 22:17 CHS concludes, 'I hear
Christ calling (you) from the throne. I hear the Spirit calling. I hear
the bride calling. I am calling as one of those who have heard the
gospel for myself. Listen, then. Oh, listen, was there ever such a
chorus of united invitation? — will you not come? "Stoop down,
and drink, and live." May God lead you so to do, for Christ's sake!
Amen.'[32]

Yet in persuading unbelievers we do not find any demeaning of
the sovereignty God. Nor was there any compromise concerning
the terms involved. 'I tell you, my Lord will never degrade his well-
beloved Son by bargaining with you about him.'[33]

3.3.9 There was a spirit of joy in the invitations

Preaching on Lord's Day evening, 6 July, 1890 he announced during
his sermon entitled Harvest Joy, that there were 82 baptised converts
to be welcomed into membership that evening, fourteen of whom
came from the girls' orphanage. This exposition and many others
ring with the fact that the most glorious thing in all the world is to
come to repentance. The angels rejoice over one sinner that repents.

---

[31] *New Park Street Pulpit*, 1855, p 24)
[32] *Metropolitan Tabernacle Pulpit*, 1900, p 353
[33] *Ibid*

The Lord's people are gladdened exceedingly by every soul that savingly believes. That sense of joy comes through in the preaching, and very much so in the invitations to come to Christ.

3.3.10 There was the sense of God himself in the invitations

During the early 1960s I came to know a trustee of Cuckfield Baptist Chapel who had lived into his 90s. As a young man he had heard Spurgeon preach. He described the unusual clarity and quality of his voice: 'It was like a golden bell, every word crystal clear.' But he remembered more vividly the sense of expectation, the total silence when the preacher appeared. This gives us a clue as we read the sermons which have been instrumental in conversions in many countries. If the sense of God and the authority of his Holy Word carries through the pages, how much more was there to be sensed the power and presence of God in the preaching and especially as sinners were persuasively reasoned with, urged, warned, counselled, appealed to, commanded, and invited to close with Christ.

Spurgeon exemplified the words of 2 Corinthians 5:20, 'We are therefore Christ's ambassadors, as though God were making his appeal through us. We implore you on Christ's behalf: Be reconciled to God.'

Are we passionate and persuasive in inviting sinners to Christ? Some may respond by saying that that is not so easy since the number of unconverted sinners attending now is minimal, if not nil most of the time, and if some attend they have heard the gospel so many times that it makes the issue more complex. We are living in barren times and have to adjust our ministries accordingly but nevertheless we need to be persuasive, passionate and unfettered in the invitations of the gospel.

If you are a preacher will you search your heart about the ten points that have been outlined? Do these features characterise your ministry? May the Holy Spirit bless and encourage you in your great calling.

Chapter 4

Spurgeon and his Social Concern

1893

On 31st January one hundred years ago, C H Spurgeon died at Mentone in the South of France fully meriting the assessment of Sir Robert Ensor who wrote that 'if native eloquence and wide popular appeal be the test, [Spurgeon] must be ranked among the greatest English preachers of any age.'[1] Spurgeon is remembered primarily as a preacher of the gospel. But he was more than that. He was also a man of social concern and social action who both directly initiated works of Christian compassion or inspired others to do so and encouraged fellow believers in their ministries among the poor and destitute.

In C H Spurgeon, the preacher of the gospel and the man of social action were one. The social action flowed from the compassion for people which was so marked a feature of his preaching. Commenting on the methods of the Roman Catholic Church in going to the poor with material relief in order to win them to the Church, Spurgeon said in a sermon preached in 1862, 'I would that we who have a purer faith, could remember a little more the intimate connection between the body and the soul. Go to the poor man and tell him of the bread of heaven, but first give him the bread of earth, for how shall he hear you with a starving body? Talk to him of the robe of Jesus' righteousness, but you will do it all the better when you have

---

[1] R C K Ensor: *England 1870–1914*, (Oxford University Press, London, 1936) p 140

91

provided a garment with which he may cover his nakedness. It seems an idle tale to a poor man if you talk to him of spiritual things and cruelly refuse to help him as to temporals. Sympathy thus expressed, may be a mighty instrument for good.'[2]

4.1   Spurgeon's London

In order to appreciate the social concern of Spurgeon it is necessary to sketch the social conditions of his day. The London in which he ministered was a rapidly growing metropolis in which many poor people lived in appalling circumstances. In 1801 the city had 1.1 million inhabitants but by 1911 that figure had grown to 7.3 million.[3] This growth in population was largely due to the migration of the rural poor to London in search of work.

Though such migration was taking place in many parts of the British Isles as an effect of the Industrial Revolution it was even more marked in the case of London which 'in every intercensal period of the nineteenth century' was percentage wise 'substantially greater (at its greatest nearly double) than the national percentage'.[4]

Urban growth then, as it still does in many parts of the world today, meant urban poverty. The dimensions of poverty in London in the latter part of the nineteenth century were chronicled by Charles Booth in the seven volumes of his Life and Labours of the People of London which appeared between 1889 and 1903. He estimated that one-quarter to one-third of the metropolis was living in poverty with regular earnings of eighteen to twenty-one shillings a week (the 'very poor' earned even less).[5]

In the overcrowded, insanitary conditions of what today we term Inner London, disease was rife and epidemics frequent. The areas of greatest poverty were those of the highest mortality. In his famous Report on the Sanitary Conditions of the Labouring Population Edwin Chadwick demonstrated that in 1839 in Bethnal Green the average age of death could be tabulated as follows:[6]

---

[2] *Christian Sympathy — A Sermon for the Lancashire Distress,* Metropolitan Tabernacle Pulpit, 1862, p 630

[3] Judith Ryder and Harold Silver: *Modern English Society — History and Structure, 1850–1970* (Methuen, London, 1970) p 35

[4] *Modern English Society — History and Structure,* p 35

[5] *Modern English Society,* p 90

[6] Cited *Modern English Society,* p 47

No. of deaths		Average age of deceased
101	Gentlemen and persons engaged in professions and their families	45 years
273	Tradesmen and their families	26 years
1,258	Mechanics, servants and labourers and their families	16 years

Friedrich Engels, Karl Marx's friend and supporter, describes St. Giles close to the fashionable West End with its narrow roads, street-markets 'in which baskets of rotting and virtually uneatable vegetables and fruit are exposed for sale', foul smells and appalling over-crowding. He pictures the narrow alleys and crowded courts, with 'hardly an unbroken window pane to be seen, the walls are crumbling, the poor posts and window frames are loose and rotten ... piles of refuse and ashes lie all over the place and the slops thrown out onto the street in pools ...'.[7]

The typical working week in 1870 was seventy hours spread over seven days.[8] Working conditions were unsafe and accidents frequent. Unemployment was often the lot of the poor especially of unskilled workers.

Though Spurgeon lived in leafy Norwood, as much for his health and sanity's sake as for any other reason, he was well aware of the insanitary and overcrowded conditions of what today we term Inner London where disease was rife and epidemics frequent. In the sermon on 'Christian Sympathy' from which I have already quoted, he pleads with his congregation to acquaint themselves with the sufferings of the poor: 'If you were to go next Monday with some City Missionary to the East End, or St Giles, or some poor district this side of the water you would say, "Dear me, I did not know that people really did suffer at this rate; I had no idea of it; or I would have given more to the poor." We want to be educated into the knowledge of our national poverty; we want to be taught and trained, to know more of what our fellow men can and do suffer. Oh! if the Christian Church knew the immorality of London, she would cry aloud to God. If but for one night you could see the harlotry and infamy; if you would but once see the rascality of London gathered into one mass, your hearts

---

[7] F Engels, *The Condition of the Working Class in England*, trans W O Henderson and W H Chaloner (Oxford 1958) p 34, quoted *Modern English Society*, p 42

[8] Ian Shaw: Charles Spurgeon and the Stockwell Orphanage: a forgotten enterprise, *Christian Graduate*, September 1976, pp 71–9

would melt with woe and bitterness, and you would bow yourselves
before God and cry unto him for this city as one mourneth for his
only son, even for his firstborn.'[9]

From February, 1854 when at the age of nineteen Spurgeon came
on a three months' trial to New Park Street Baptist Church in Southwark until his death nearly 40 years later he ministered in the teeming
metropolis with its extremes of wealth and poverty, power and pow-
erlessness, beauty and ugliness.

4.2 Spurgeon's Social Concern — its roots

Spurgeon's social concern has more than one root; in fact, in my judgment, it has several. The most obvious root and the most important
is, of course, his biblical faith. For Spurgeon, it was axiomatic that
faith in God's Son must lead to compassion towards one's fellow men
and women and their children. For him compassion was empty unless it led to action to relieve the sufferings of the poor and needy.

But I wish to examine the roots of Spurgeon's social concern in
what is, I think, a more illuminating way than simply to start with
his understanding of the Bible. Of course the roots which I identify
intertwine in the life of the man and, more than that, they tend to
nourish each other.

First there is Spurgeon's upbringing. Born on June 19, 1834 in
the small Essex town of Kelvedon, at the age of fourteen months he
was taken to the home of his father's parents in the small secluded
village of Stamborne. There he spent the following five years and
much other time throughout his boyhood for a reason not hard to
discover, he being the eldest of seventeen children! We might say
of Spurgeon that he was town-born but country bred. To be country
bred meant an acquaintance with rural poverty, with frequent deaths
from consumption (tuberculosis) and with the desolating effects of
alcoholism upon families.

It is significant that Spurgeon's immensely popular little work was
entitled *John Ploughman's Talk or Plain Advice to Plain People*.[10]
Only a countryman at heart could have chosen such a title and have
adopted what the author termed 'the rustic style' (preface). John

---

[9] *op cit,* p 632

[10] *John Ploughman's Talk* published by Passmore and Alabaster, London, went
through many printings. My personal copy has, '300TH THOUSAND' on its title
page

Ploughman's remarks on the operation of the Poor Law, especially no doubt the 1834 Poor Law Amendment Act which required that the lot of those received into the workhouse be worse off than that of the lowest labourer outside, reflect Spurgeon's own knowledge of the sufferings of the rural poor: 'I wish our governors would not break up so many poor men's homes by that abominably heartless poor law. It is far more fit for a set of Red Indians than Englishmen. A Hampshire carter told me the other day that his wife and children were all in the union, and his home broken up, because of the cruel working of the poor law. He had eight little ones and his wife to keep on nine shillings a week, with rent to pay out of it; on this he could not keep body and soul together; now, if the parish had allowed him a mere trifle, a loaf or two and a couple of shillings a week, he would have jogged on, but no, not a penny out of the house; they might all die of starvation unless they would all go into the workhouse. So with many bitter tears and heartaches, the poor soul had to sell his few bits of furniture, and he is now a houseless man, and yet he is a good hard-working fellow, and served one master for nearly twenty years.'

John Ploughman goes on to say that he wants the Poor Law system abolished: 'Home is the pillar of the British Empire and ought not to be knocked to pieces by these unchristian laws. I wish I was an orator and could talk politics, I would not care a rush for Whigs or Tories, but I would stand up like a lion for the poor man's home, which, let me tell the Lords and Commons, is as dear to him as their great palaces are to them and sometimes dearer.'[11]

A second root of Spurgeon's social concern is to be found in his political convictions. Though he broke with Gladstone over his proposal of Home Rule for Ireland, Spurgeon was an unashamed Liberal who was not prepared to hide his political creed under a pastoral bushel. For his honesty in not concealing his political views, Spurgeon was roundly criticised by some as descending, 'From his high and lofty position as a servant of God, and preacher of the everlasting gospel, into the defiled arena of party politics', as one correspondent put it. To him Spurgeon replied on March 22, 1880, 'Your letter amuses me, because you are so evidently a rank Tory, and so hearty in your political convictions that, in spite of your religious scruples, you must needs interfere in politics, and write to me. If there is anything defiling in it, you are certainly over head and ears.

---

[11]'Home', chapter XIII in *John Ploughman's Talk*, pp 95–96

However, dear sir, I thank you for your kindness in wishing to put me right, and I can assure you that I vote as devoutly as I pray, and I feel it to be part of my love to God and to my neighbour to try to turn out the Government whom your letter would lead me to let alone.' He assured a member of the Plymouth Brethren who had warned him to, 'Leave politics to the devil and mortify the old man,' that he was doing precisely that, since, 'My old man is a Tory, and so I make him vote Liberal.'[12]

However, Spurgeon was no uncritical party loyalist. Replying to a letter from his old Cambridge friend, Mr J S Watts, he wrote in a letter dated June 19, 1880: 'I belong to the party which knows no party. To cheapen beer, to confirm the opium course, to keep in office the shedders of blood, and to put Papists to the front, are things I never expected from Mr Gladstone; but "cursed be the man that trusteth in man". Yet I am a Gladstonite despite all this.'[13] As a Dissenter and a Liberal, Spurgeon stood against the power and privilege of the political establishment which found its expression in the Tory party. He spoke out against the assumed airs of the wealthy and their expectation of deference from the poor. 'When people come out of church, what a gradation there is! Have I not seen this in many a country village how, first of all, the squire goes out, and then the bailiff follows, and then the poor people curtsey and bow and show their abject servitude and serfdom. And all this in a Christian land! In our Dissenting places of worship what stiffness there is; what rustling of the silks up one aisle and what quietude of the cottons in another!'[14] He was emphatically upon the side of those who were excluded from the corridors of power because they were Dissenters in religion and as emphatically against those who looked down upon the poor from bastions of privilege acquired either by inheritance or wealth.

A third root of social concern sprang from his belief in the voluntary principle. According to this principle the Christian church is meant to be distinct from the state, a company of believers as distinguished from a population of citizens. As a voluntaryist in religion, Spurgeon was a strong opponent of religious establishment. He was a keen supporter of the Liberation Society, which was formed in 1844 as 'The British Anti-State Church Association' and renamed 'The So-

[12] *C H Spurgeon's Autobiography*, compiled from his diary, letters and records, by his wife and his private secretary (Passmore and Alabaster, London 1900) vol IV, 1858, p 125
[13] *Autobiography*, p 126
[14] *Christian Sympathy*, *Metropolitan Tabernacle Pulpit*, 1862, p 632

ciety for the Liberation of Religion from State Patronage and Control' in 1853. Thereafter it became known as 'The Liberation Society' and its meetings were quite often held at the Metropolitan Tabernacle.

At a time of rapid population movement from the countryside to the towns and cities of Great Britain, the parish system proved ill adapted to meet the spiritual and social needs of the urban masses. It appeared to many Nonconformists, Spurgeon among them, that the voluntary principle provided for a much more flexible approach.

The Metropolitan Tabernacle was, both in Spurgeon's own eyes and in the eyes of thousands of Nonconformists, a telling illustration of the power of voluntarism. Its various institutions, with the Pastors' College and the Stockwell Orphanage the most prominent, demonstrated that without State aid, vital needs could be met by direct appeals to believing hearts and consecrated purses. Voluntarism, Spurgeon believed, was the best instrument of Christian charity.

Another root of Spurgeon's social concern is to be traced to the ministry of the church of which he was the pastor. Though the members of the church were not, it would seem, drawn from the lower working class to any great extent, there were certainly many artisans in the church as well as tradesmen and salaried people. There were also many working class people in the mission halls connected with the Tabernacle. Furthermore many poor people resorted to Spurgeon for financial help and through the Orphanage he was intimately acquainted with and moved by the plight of the poor. Again with Spurgeon's encouragement, many Tabernacle members were involved in the work of the mission halls located in the poor districts. Yet others were engaged in teaching in Ragged Schools. So Spurgeon's social concern was nourished both through direct and indirect contact with the poor.

As I have affirmed at the beginning, the most important root of Spurgeon's social concern was the Bible. As he read, meditated upon, preached and practised the Book of books, his social concern grew and found expression in a network of Christian enterprises of which he was the centre, though aided by many who worked heartily with him.

Spurgeon did not read his Bible as a pietist who separated religion off into a private realm removed from social and political life. For Spurgeon the Christian religion is a 'present religion' to use the title of a sermon he preached in 1858 on 1 John 3:2, 'Beloved *now* are we the sons of God'. He would permit no escape into other-

worldliness to avoid the duties of the present moment, as if heaven
is best anticipated by ignoring present needs. 'Religion ... must be a
present thing; we need not to talk of walking righteously, and soberly,
in the world to come —

"There all is pure, and all is clear,

There all is joy and love."

There will be no duty to discharge between the tradesman and
the customer, between the debtor and the creditor, between the father and his child, between the husband and the wife, in heaven, for
all these relationships shall have passed away. Religion must be intended for this life; the duties of it cannot be practised, unless they
are practised here.'[15]
For Spurgeon, love of God and love of neighbour demolished
the convenient distinction between the sacred and the secular which
many make to justify a concentration on heavenly rewards to the neglect of earthly duties. In preaching upon Christians' calling to let
their lights shine in the world, he declared; 'God grant that the day
may come when the mischievous division between secular and religious things shall be no more heard of, for in all things Christians are
to glorify God ...'[16]
Spurgeon in consequence was no dualist exalting the needs of
the soul over the demands of the body. In a sermon entitled 'Camp
Law and Camp Life' based on Deuteronomy 23:14 and printed in
Metropolitan Tabernacle Pulpit, 1890, Spurgeon begins thus: 'I will
scarcely allude to the context, which you ought to notice at home,
but I must say as much as this: *the Lord cared for the cleanliness of
his people while they were in the wilderness*, literally so; and this text
is connected with a sanitary regulation of the wisest possible kind.
What I admire is that God the glorious, the all-holy, should stoop
to legislate about such things. Such attention was very necessary for
health and even for life, and the Lord in condescending to it, con-
veys a severe rebuke to Christian people who have been careless in
matters respecting health and cleanliness. Saintly souls should not

[15]'A Present Religion', *New Park Street Pulpit*, (Passmore and Alabaster, London
1892) vol IV, 1858, p 253
[16]Quoted by David Nelson Duke: 'Charles Haddon Spurgeon: Social Concern Ex-
ceeding an Individualistic, Self-Help Ideology', *Baptist History and Heritage*, October
1987, p 48. The quotation is from 'The Candle' in *Metropolitan Tabernacle Pulpit*,
1882, p226

be lodged in filthy bodies. God takes note of matters which persons who are falsely spiritual speak of as beneath their observation. If the Lord cares for such things, we must not neglect them.'[17]

In the light of such an holistic emphasis we are not surprised to learn that in 1885 Spurgeon arranged a meeting at Haddon Hall Mission, one of the mission halls connected with the Tabernacle, for those interested in the religious, social and sanitary conditions of the district (i.e. Bermondsey).[18] Among the matters considered at that meeting were overcrowding, unemployment, immorality, drink, profanity.[19] The *Sword and Trowel* from which this account is taken noted that, 'Sixteen people and two cats might be found living in one room.'[20]

A dominant theme in Spurgeon's biblical social concern is sympathy. Himself a man of deep sympathy, moved to the depths of his being as he preached to sinners and ministered to the afflicted, he emphasised sympathy as integral to social concern. On Sunday morning, 9 November, 1862, he preached a sermon on Job 30:25, 'Did I not weep for him that was in trouble? Was not my soul grieved for the poor?' The occasion of the sermon was 'The Lancashire Distress', the plight of the workers in the Lancashire cotton mills who were made unemployed because of the drying up of supplies of American cotton as a result of the ravages of the civil war then raging in the United States. Spurgeon recognises 'the generous feeling towards the poor and suffering that exists in many an unregenerate heart'. Yet he insists that sympathy is especially a Christian duty. 'The Christian is a king; it becometh not a king to be meanly caring for himself ... The Christian's sympathy should ever be of the widest character, because he serves a God of infinite love ... To me a follower of Jesus means a friend of man. A Christian is a philanthropist by profession, and generous by the force of grace; wide as the reign of sorrow is the stretch of his love, and where he cannot help he pities still.'[21]

Spurgeon next emphasises that sympathy is essential to our usefulness as Christians. 'I know that a man in the ministry who cannot feel, had much better resign his office. We have heard some hold forth the doctrines of grace, as if they were a nauseous medicine and

[17]'Camp Law and Camp Life', *Metropolitan Tabernacle Pulpit*, 1880, p 661

[18]Eric W Hayden, *A Centennial History of Spurgeon's Tabernacle*, London. Clifford Frost Limited 1962, p 79, citing *Sword and Trowel*, 1885 p 344

[19]*Sword and Trowel*, cited Hayden p 344

[20]*Sword and Trowel*, cited Hayden p 348

[21]*Metropolitan Tabernacle Pulpit*, 1862, pp 628–9

men were to be forced to drink thereof by hard words and violent abuse ... To such men heaven and hell, death and eternity, are mere themes for oratory, but not subjects for emotion. The man who will do most good must throw himself into his words; and put his whole being into intense communion with the truth which he utters.'[22] Sympathy is not, however to be the preserve of preachers. It should mark out every disciple of Christ. Compassion in preachers should beget compassion in hearers. 'When they feel that there is a caring heart within the preacher, then they give the more earnest heed to the things whereof we speak. You Sunday school teachers, you must have warm hearts or you will be of little use to your children. You street-preachers, city missionaries, Bible women, and tract distributors, you who in any way seek to serve your Lord — a heart, a heart, a tender heart, a flaming heart, a heart saturated with intense sympathy, this, when sanctified by the Holy Spirit, will give success in your endeavours.'[23]

Lack of sympathy arises from selfishness and ignorance, the first thing often being the mother of the second. Spurgeon could be accused of neither, for he gave away most of what could have been a sizable fortune accruing from the royalties on his published works, and was well informed about the plight of the poor.

Though he did not idealize the poor he was prepared, much more than many preachers today, to see them as victims of man's inhumanity to man. Preaching on the parable of the Good Samaritan in 1877 on behalf of the Hospitals of London, he points out that, *'Certain paths of life are peculiarly subject to affliction.'* The way which led from Jerusalem to Jericho was always infested with robbers. Jerome tells us that it was called the "bloody way" on account of the frequent highway robberies and murders which were committed ...'

Spurgeon then applies the point with great force: 'Years ago there were many trades in which from want of precaution death slew its thousands. I thank God that sanitary and precautionary laws are better regarded and men's lives are thought somewhat more precious. Yet still there are ways of life which may each be called "the bloody way": pursuits which are necessary to the community, but highly dangerous to those who follow them. Our mines, our railways and our seas show a terrible toll of suffering and death. Long hours in ill ventilated work-rooms are accountable for thousands of lives,

---

[22] *Metropolitan Tabernacle Pulpit,* 1862, p 629
[23] *Metropolitan Tabernacle Pulpit,* 1862, p 629

and so are stinted wages, which prevent a sufficiency of food from being procured. When I think of the multitude of our working people in this city who have to live in close, unhealthy rooms, crowded together in lanes and courts where the air is stagnant, I do not hesitate to say that much of the road trodden by the poor in London is as much deserving of the name of the way of blood as the road from Jerusalem to Jericho.'[24]

These are pointed political statements which demonstrate the falsity of Horton Davies' remark that 'Spurgeon took the pietistical view that preachers should keep politics out of the pulpit'.[25] Spurgeon may not have been a founder member of the Fabian Society as another well-known Baptist minister, John Clifford, was but it is simply incorrect to class Spurgeon as a non-political, pietistic preacher concerned exclusively with the salvation of souls.

Though it would not be accurate to characterise Spurgeon as maintaining that God exercises a preferential option towards the poor he certainly drew attention to what he regarded as, 'an undeniable fact, that God has been pleased for the most part to plant his grace in the soil of poverty.'[26] In the sermon from which this quotation is taken Spurgeon gives us a glimpse of pressures upon him to relieve the wants of the poor: 'Some of us have pretty good need to remember the poor. I am sure I have, for I have about ten times as many poor people come to me every day as I can possibly relieve.'[27]

Spurgeon was not unaware of what a contemporary American writer, Gibson Winter, has termed 'the suburban captivity of the churches'. In a sermon preached at the Metropolitan Tabernacle after its opening in 1860 Spurgeon made this observation: 'You know that, in the City of London itself, there is scarcely one Dissenting place of worship. The reason for giving up most of the chapels or transferring the church to the suburbs, is that all the respectable people live out of town, and of course they are the folk to look after. They will not stop in London, they will go out a few miles and take villas; and therefore the best thing is to use the endowment, which belonged to the old chapel, in building a new place of worship somewhere in

[24]'The Good Samaritan', *Metropolitan Tabernacle Pulpit*, 1877, pp 351–2

[25]Horton Davies, 'Worship and Theology in England', p 345 cited by Patricia Stallings Kruppa, *Charles Haddon Spurgeon — A Preacher's Progress,* Garland Publishing Company, 1982, p 351

[26]'The Duty of Remembering the Poor', sermon on Galatians 2:10, *New Park Street Pulpit*, 1856, p 366

[27]*New Park Street Pulpit*, 1856, p 366

the suburbs where it can be maintained. 'No doubt' it is said, 'the poor ought to be looked after; but we had better leave them to an inferior order of workers — the city missionaries will do for them, or we can send them a few street preachers ...'

Now my experience of the poor of Christ's flock teaches me that all this kind of talk is folly. If there are any people who love the cause of God better than others, I believe it is the poor, when the grace of God takes real possession of their heart.'[28]

One other aspect of Spurgeon's biblical social concern remains to be noted: his attitude to war. Though no pacifist, Spurgeon frequently emphasised the horrors of war, often in a jingoistic climate of opinion, when it was by no means popular to do so. War was sin not only because of the suffering it caused, but also it went against God's scriptural commands. To him war was 'a great crime — murder on a huge scale — and little less than hell let loose among men. "Thou shalt not kill" is as much a divine commandment as "Thou shalt not commit adultery". No one supposed that adultery on a great scale would be right: then why should killing be?'[29]

Spurgeon was prepared to oppose the 'periodical war madness', as he termed it, which from time to time seared the nation during the heyday of British imperialism. Many of his countrymen, he said, called for 'a warlike policy as loudly as if it involved no slaughter, and were rather a boon to mankind than an unmitigated curse. A mysterious argument, founded upon the protection of certain mythical 'British interests' is set up as an excuse, but the fact is that the national bulldog wants to fix his teeth into somebody's leg, and growls because he does not quite see how to do it. The fighting instinct is asking to be gratified and waxes violent because it is denied indulgence,'[30]

As Spurgeon said, 'It is the Christian's duty always to have war with war. To have bitterness in our hearts against any man who lives is to serve Satan.' 'War! War! War!'[31]

The roots of Spurgeon's social concern then are several, as we

---

[28] *Autobiography*, vol III, p 2 (Passmore and Alabaster, London, 1899)

[29] *'A Letter About His Other Letter*, by John Ploughman, Sword and Trowel, September 1870, p 433, cited by David Nelson Duke: *Asking the Right Questions About War — A Lesson From C H Spurgeon*, Evangelical Quarterly, vol 61 1 (1989), 71–80, on page 76

[30] 'Periodical War Madness', *Sword and Trowel*, April, 1878, p 146 cited Duke *op cit* p 77

[31] *New Park Street Pulpit*, 1859, p 204

have seen: in his upbringing, his political convictions, his belief in the voluntary principle, the ministry of the church of which he was pastor, and the Bible. The Bible ranked first in importance, of course, but the other roots must be given their proper weight if Spurgeon's social concern is to be appreciated in its various dimensions.

4.3 Spurgeon's Social Concern — its various expressions

As the membership of the Metropolitan Tabernacle grew to over five thousand there was, of course, the danger that many members would be content to occupy a seat on Sundays and do little else. Spurgeon was well aware of this danger. His way of counteracting this was both simple and effective. Let him describe it in his own words:

> 'Every member who joins my church is expected to do something for his fellow creatures. After I have had a talk with him and satisfied myself as to his sincerity, I say to him: "My good fellow, you seem to be a converted man, and I hope that you are truly a Christian; but, suppose you join the church, what are you going to do for your fellow men? If, after you are admitted, you will do nothing for them, I cannot help it; we have made a bad bargain, that's all; but no one shall enter with my will who does not promise beforehand to undertake, if at all possible, some useful work for the benefit of others." In many cases the idea never seems to have struck them that this was an essential part of Christian duty. It makes them think of what they can do and in most cases they profess their readiness to do whatever I think would be most useful!'[32]

The effectiveness with which Spurgeon harnessed and directed the energies of the Tabernacle members can be seen in the vast number of agencies which emanated from the church as well as Sunday School work both within the Tabernacle and in missions connected

---

[32] Quoted in an address on *Service* by Robert Wilson Black in Henry Townsend, *Robert Wilson Black*, Carey Kingsgate Press, London 1954, p 103. The source of Spurgeon's words is given as 'an interview with a representative of the *Pall Mall Gazette*,' but no date is mentioned.

with the Tabernacle. These works are fully listed in chapters 10 and 11 of Arnold Dallimore's biography of Spurgeon published by the Banner of Truth in 1985.

Kathleen Heasman is correct to point out that the Metropolitan Tabernacle was exceptional. There is no parallel, I think, in British ecclesiastical history, for one church originating so many and varied organisations. 'All this', she writes, 'was exceptional and due to Spurgeon's popularity which placed at his disposal not only a much wider choice of leaders but also much larger funds than were usually available to the ordinary church.'[33] Nonetheless it took a man who was more than a great preacher to have a vision of human need — spiritual, physical, social — and to motivate believers to respond to it in love and good works. Furthermore, it took a man who could impart vision and then delegate to others (such as his brother James) the implementation and outworking of it.

I do not propose to describe the founding and development of the Stockwell Orphanage (now Spurgeon's Child Care) in any detail, as it has received adequate treatment elsewhere particularly by Dr Ian Shaw and Paul Mersh.[34] Begun in 1867 with a gift of £20,000 from the widow of an Anglican minister, Mrs Anne Hillyard, originally for boys but later enlarged to care for girls as well, it was a single-church work during Spurgeon's life-time. It was Spurgeon's desire, only to be imperfectly realised, that the Orphanage should consist of family sized groups. In the November 1867 edition of *Sword and Trowel*, he explained his thinking to its readers:

> 'Theoretically the family plan is promising because it approximates to the way of our Heavenly Father, who has not sent us into this world in vast companies to sleep in long wards and to live in a crowd, but has billetted us in our own sweet homes, where brothers and sisters, and parents and children are.'[35]

For a number of reasons, Dr Ian Shaw points out, the 'family plan' was not fulfilled as it might have been. The houses were single-sex

---

[33] Kathleen Heasman *Evangelicals in Action — An Appraisal of their Social Work in the Victorian Era*, (Geoffrey Bles, London, 1962), p 52

[34] Ian Shaw, 'Charles Spurgeon and the Stockwell Orphanage: a forgotten enterprise', *Christian Graduate*, September 1976, pp 71–79. Paul Mersh: 'The origins and functioning of the Stockwell Orphanage'. Dissertation submitted towards the MA Historical Studies degree in Humanities (C.N.A.A.) at Thames Polytechnic

[35] Paul Mersh, *op cit* p10, quoting *Sword and Trowel*, November 1867 p 512

and catered for an average of more than forty children. They were not staffed by married couples but by a matron and assistant matron, despite a Trustees decision, 'That it is very desirable that a man and wife be in charge of each house and that all the men employed except the schoolmaster, be the husband of one of the matrons.'[36] Also, probably for reasons of economy, uniformity of dress tended to emerge, a trend which seems to have accelerated after Spurgeon's death, despite Spurgeon's frequently stated view that, 'Orphanhood is a child's misfortune and should not be treated as though it were his fault. In a garb which is the symbol of dependence, it is difficult if not impossible for an orphan to preserve a feeling of self-respect.'[37]

It is easy in the light of contemporary thinking about child care to criticise Spurgeon and the Orphanage Trustees but it needs to be appreciated what an advance the Stockwell Orphanage was when set in the context of the age in which Spurgeon lived. As Paul Mersh points out, 'The prevailing form of provision for orphaned children at this time was the workhouse,'[38] and even Müller in Bristol still used barrack type accommodation. It was a friend of Spurgeon, Thomas Barnardo (who quite probably borrowed the idea from Spurgeon) who was to open 'cottages' at Barkingside in Essex in which house parents cared for small family units. It was not in fact until the 1950s that Spurgeon's Orphanage, as it had by then become, adopted the house-parent system in its purpose-built homes in Birchington, subsequent to the publication of the Curtis Report which had recommended it for all child care institutions. Paul Mersh is right to see the Stockwell Orphanage as representing, 'A sort of half way house between the near work house arrangements of Müller and the house parents run cottages of Barnardo.'[39]

Spurgeon was deeply concerned for the spiritual well-being of the children. He desired to see them converted and becoming useful members of churches and society. In this he was not disappointed although it would seem that over the years the numbers of conversions were not large in comparison with the total number of children in the orphanage (though it is more than likely that some would have been converted after leaving at fourteen). Of one child, Comber, converted at Stockwell, subsequently trained for the ministry in the Pas-

---

[36] Cited by Ian Shaw, *op cit* p 76 from *Stockwell Orphanage: Minute Books*, No.1, 1867–76

[37] Cited by Ian Shaw, p 76 from *Stockwell Orphanage: Annual Report* 1889

[38] *op cit* p 12

[39] *op cit* p 12

tor's College, Spurgeon movingly says: 'Comber went to the Congo and so took the short route to heaven.'

Though the Orphanage had its own school, which did not come under the supervision of the London County Council until 1922, and the Metropolitan Tabernacle did as well for a number of years,[40] Spurgeon's hope that 'a grammar school of the highest order' should be established to counteract episcopal influence over our children' was never realised.[41] By 1868 it is clear that Spurgeon's attitude towards a national education system had changed. As a champion of voluntaryism his first response to the idea of such a system was negative. However, in practice a voluntary system worked to the disadvantage of dissenters because they would not provide the number of schools needed. Therefore Spurgeon proposed in 1868 that a national system of education be established which would provide teaching of a non-sectarian character: 'We should like to see a system of universal application which would give a sound education to children and leave the religious training to the home and the agencies of the church of Christ.'[42] Spurgeon opposed the idea of secular education advocated by the militant National Education League which wanted even Bible reading excluded from schools. He worked to get nonconformists to support the provisions of the 1870 Education Act, though he recognised that it was a compromise, being an attempt to fill the gaps in the existing system.

The other feature of the educational work of the Tabernacle deserves mention. In 1862 evening classes were begun, the syllabus being designed to suit those of sixteen years and upwards. No fees were charged, Spurgeon paying out of his own pocket. Science, English Language and Literature, Elementary Mathematics and Bookkeeping were taught. Pitman's Shorthand was soon added. In providing evening classes the Metropolitan Tabernacle pioneered a path which was later followed by secular bodies. Eric Hayden points out that when the London School Board began to explore the possibility of providing evening adult educational facilities its committee turned to the Metropolitan Tabernacle for advice.[43]

Spurgeon was not only the initiator of organisations; he was also the supporter of many charitable works begun by others. He often preached for the Ragged School Union, whose schools sought to pro-

[40] W Hayden, *op cit* pp 76–7

[41] *Sword and Trowel*, 1866, cited Shaw, *op cit* p 71

[42] *Sword and Trowel*, cited by Kruppa, *op cit* p 323

[43] Eric Hayden, *op cit* pp 76–7

vide a rudimentary education for the children of the poor and very poor. He was president of the 'Female Servants' Home Society', which had four hostels accommodating about a hundred servants. He frequently preached in support of hospitals and he also preached on behalf of a society which campaigned for shorter hours for shop assistants.

In a sermon on the Good Samaritan, he defended himself from what today would be a charge of preaching the social gospel; 'There are certain persons in the world who will not allow the preacher to speak about anything but those doctrinal statements concerning the way of salvation which are known as "the gospel" ... We do not stand in awe of such criticism, for we clearly perceive that our Lord Jesus Christ himself would very frequently have come under it. Read the Sermon on the Mount and judge whether certain people would be content to hear the like of it preached to them on the Sabbath'.[44] Spurgeon's own deep sense of compassion clearly made him broad in his sympathies.

Spurgeon has been criticised from various standpoints. Though his social concern cannot be denied, neo-Marxists have suggested that he was at fault for not being concerned with the restructuring of society. He is seen as preaching only a message of individual regeneration and as therefore being individualistic.[45] However, it is not correct to infer that, because he emphasised personal responsibility before God and called upon individuals to repent and believe the gospel, he was uninterested in changing society for the better. All the evidence is against such an inference.

Furthermore it is anachronistic to charge Spurgeon with a lack of interest in restructuring society. The means to do so were simply not in the hands of dissenters, whereas the clamant needs of London cried out for immediate relief. It is also worth making the point that the twentieth century has witnessed human suffering on an unparalleled scale which is the direct outcome of attempts to restructure society from top to bottom. Spurgeon has also been accused of, on occasion, allowing himself 'to equate poverty with vice'.[46] While his language *could* be pressed to support such a conclusion the overall tenor of Spurgeon's utterances on the subject of the poor certainly

---

[44] *Metropolitan Tabernacle Pulpit*, 1877, pp 349–50

[45] David Nelson Duke makes this charge but he effectively refutes it in the rest of his article. See note 16 for bibliographical details

[46] Patricia Stallings Kruppa, *C H Spurgeon — A Preacher's Progress*, (Garland Publishing, 1982), p 165

cannot. Spurgeon is surely on firm biblical ground when, on the one hand, he insists that some poverty is the direct result of personal responsibility and, on the other, that much poverty is the direct result of the oppressing of the weak by the powerful. The Bible condemns both the sluggard and the rich who oppress the poor. Thus Spurgeon says both that, 'Very much of the poverty about us is the result of idleness, intemperance, improvidence and sin,'[47] and, 'Work-people ... are often sorely oppressed in their wages, and have to work themselves to death's door to earn a pittance.'[48]

It could be argued that Spurgeon tied his social philosophy too closely to Liberalism but then so too, did the great majority of Dissenters. The union of the non-conformist conscience with the Liberal Party may have been a temporary phenomenon but while it lasted much good, I would argue, was accomplished.

What surely stands out in Spurgeon is his immense compassion. Moved with compassion as he preached the gospel of the grace of God to sinners he showed a like compassion to the poor and needy. A gospel man he was first and foremost but he was large of heart in a way which few of us are.

His preaching was so owned of God that during his ministry the Metropolitan Tabernacle grew to over five thousand members but they were not allowed to dwell at ease in Zion. Spurgeon could open eyes to see need, enlarge hearts to feel it, and empty pockets to meet it. He expected his people to be generous and he was not disappointed. Could we not have greater expectations of our people than we do?

Spurgeon enjoyed the support not only of his church but of many members of the Christian public in a way that no preacher does today. It will not do, however, to argue that he was unique and had unique backing. For he would surely reply, 'My God is your God and he requires that we love him and our neighbour as ourselves. This stands written for all time.' So one hundred years after the death of Spurgeon we need to do some heart searching — that we are more often than not comfortable Christians rather than compassionate ones. We surely must become in ourselves and in our churches generous by the force of grace', deep in our sympathies and wide in our concerns for 'wide as the reign of sorrow' should be 'the stretch of our love'.

---

[47] Kruppa, *op cit* p 165
[48] *Metropolitan Tabernacle Pulpit*, 1877, p 351

Our duty is plain: 'He has shown you, O man, what is good; And what does the Lord require of you but to do justly, to love mercy, and to walk humbly with [our] God' (Micah 6:8).

Our religion should be obvious: 'Pure and undefiled religion before God and the Father is this: to visit orphans and widows in their trouble, and to keep ourselves unspotted from the world' (James 1:27).

Chapter 5

C H Spurgeon and the Downgrade Controversy

In seeking to understand and to evaluate the Downgrade controversy it is important to relate it to the general theological background of Spurgeon's day because the controversy itself was, in part at least, a reaction to a movement in theology which was affecting practically all denominations, not merely the Baptist. Having sketched in this background, we shall then look at the Baptist Union, and afterwards we shall describe the course of the controversy. In the latter part of this chapter we shall consider the main issues in the Downgrade controversy, and finally we shall attempt to draw out some relevant conclusions.

5.1 The Theological Background

The Downgrade controversy broke out in a period of theological decline. Calvinism, the system of theology that had been common to both Congregationalists and Particular Baptists, had entered upon days of weakness. Whilst it remained inscribed in the confessional statements of both denominations and in the trust deeds of hundreds of churches, in practice it was being modified and in many instances abandoned altogether. However, it was not so much that the doctrines of grace as articulated by reformed theology were being explicitly denied, as that they were not being definitely preached; it was

111

not that they were being openly attacked, but rather they were being quietly ignored.

The decline of Calvinism had a distant genesis. Theologically one effect of the Evangelical Revival of the eighteenth century, and certainly of the 1858–9 revival, was the undermining of the Calvinism of the confessional standards. Emphasis came to be put on evangelism at home and abroad, but to the neglect of serious theological thinking. In England serious theological study seemed to be the prerogative of Anglicans who were emphatically not Calvinists. In Scotland, however, the outlook was brighter because of the activities of men such as Cunningham, Buchanan, Smeaton and Bannerman.

In the life of the Churches, doctrine tended to be depreciated in favour of winning the masses for Christ. Stress was placed upon practical Christianity with the implication that doctrine was relatively unimportant. There was a growing unwillingness to define the Gospel; it was said that Christ must be preached, but few stopped to ask what sort of Christ was being proclaimed. The Christian life was increasingly separated from Christian doctrine, it being assumed that doctrine did not really shape experience, but rather that doctrine was but the formulation of data provided by Christian experience. Thus 'experience' tended to be made the norm, whilst doctrines, however greatly they conflicted, were viewed as insights based upon experience. The emphasis was shifting from what God had revealed to what man could formulate.

It is the great merit of Willis B Glover's book, *Evangelical Nonconformists and Higher Criticism in the Nineteenth Century*,[1] that it traces the effects of the decline of Calvinism in preparing the way for the widespread acceptance of the naturalists positions of higher criticism. With the decline of Calvinism there came about the dissolution of a coherent, well-knit, body of doctrine. 'The general decline of Calvinism', writes Glover, 'was not the result of any rival theological system. Its place was taken by the widest variety of theological speculation singularly lacking in intellectual vigour, and in relationship to any well developed system of basic ideas.'[2] In short, the decline of Calvinism left a theological vacuum which was soon filled with myriad streams of theological ideas. R W Dale wrote in *The Congregationalist* in 1877: 'We have no theological system in the sense that Calvinism was the theological system of the Puritans of the sixteenth

---

[1] London, The Independent Press, 1954
[2] *Op cit*, pp 92–3

and seventeenth centuries. It may be doubted whether for a long time to come any such system is likely to be constructed that will secure the universal adhesion of Congregationalists. What may be described as the Congregational theological tradition has been broken. We have no longer a common theological life ... '[3] Whilst the decline of Calvinism was not, I think, so rapid and pronounced among the Baptists, there were nonetheless among them strong forces at work hastening its dissolution.

Without attempting to trace all the theological effects of the decline of Calvinism, we shall be content to draw attention to two important areas of doctrine in which the lessening vigour of Reformed theology opened the way for speculation. In both areas Spurgeon attacked ideas which were coming to be frequently mooted and freely preached among nonconformists.

The first area was that of the future life. The orthodox doctrine declared that the wicked who die impenitent are subjected to the eternal punishment of God. It was laid under attack in three ways: (i) along the lines of 'conditional immortality', (ii) by teaching the universal salvation of all creation, and (iii) by the concept of future probation.

Ever since the publication of Edward White's *Life in Christ* in 1846 the doctrine of eternal punishment had been an issue among nonconformists. White, a Congregational minister, claimed Scriptural support for the position that only those who do not believe are annihilated, either at death or following the day of judgement. As a consequence of this view the impenitent sinner escapes eternal punishment, which White declared to be unjust and unworthy of God. Spurgeon did not hesitate to oppose White's teaching from his own pulpit, and in the religious press, including his own magazine, *Sword and Trowel*. White himself acknowledged the effectiveness of Spurgeon's opposition in an anniversary sermon preached at St. Paul's Chapel, Kentish Town, in 1882. 'No one', he said, 'yields to me in hearty admiration and affection for the Rev Charles Spurgeon. But his refusal to listen to the doctrine of life in Christ has formed a more serious obstacle to its popular diffusion than that of any other man living during the last twenty years.'[4]

---

[3] Quoted Glover, *Ibid*, p 93

[4] *Spurgeon Scrapbooks*, VI, p 56. This series of scrapbooks, which was almost certainly compiled by Spurgeon's secretary, the Rev J W Harrald, is now in the possession of Spurgeon's College, South Norwood Hill, London, SE 25. It contains much valuable material chiefly in the form of personal letters and newspaper cuttings.

As far back as 1860, Spurgeon was involved in a controversy which in large measure also turned upon the question of future punishment. The Rev J Howard Hinton, M.A., a veteran Baptist minister and a former secretary of the Baptist Union, had published two articles in the 'Baptist Magazine' for March and April, 1860, under the title, 'Strictures on some passages in the Rev J B Brown's "Divine Life in Man"'. J Baldwin Brown, a Congregationalist minister, propagated the ideas of F D Maurice, who in 1853 had affirmed that 'eternal' punishment did not mean something which lasted forever, with no hope of repentance on the part of the sinner. Hinton's articles were afterwards reprinted and issued as a pamphlet. The reviews of the 'Strictures' published in the 'Freeman', the semi-official organ of the Baptist denomination, was considered by Spurgeon and several other prominent Baptist ministers to be of so unsatisfactory a character that seven of them signed a joint-protest, which was published in the 'Freeman' on April 11th. Among the other signatories was Joseph Angus, who was to take the opposite view to Spurgeon on the Downgrade controversy. We quote two passages from the letter. The first illustrates the widespread fear that the undermining of the doctrine of future punishment would have serious consequences for the preaching of the Gospel. 'We do not hesitate to avow our conviction that both the principles and their consequences, whether categorically stated, or involved in a metaphor, go to subvert the whole scheme of God's moral government as revealed in the sacred Scriptures, and with it those precious truths which cluster round the cross and centre in it, and which, for that reason, are most distinctive of the Gospel, and most fundamental to it.'[5]

The second quotation expresses the persuasion of the authors of the letter that 'the doctrines of grace' are vital to the spiritual health of the Churches. 'Above all, we desire affectionately to caution those in the ministry, who are younger than ourselves (C H S was 26!) against that style of preaching which, under the pretentious affectation of being intellectual, grows unashamed of the old and vulgar doctrines of man's guilt, as well as of his total depravity, of Christ's atonement and satisfaction for sin, of justification by the imputation of His righteousness through faith, of the new birth by the agency of the Holy Spirit, and, in a word, of that scheme of dogmatic Christian truth which is popularly known under the designation of "the doc-

---

[5] C H Spurgeon: *The Autobiography*, vol II (London, Passmore & Alabaster, 1898), p 271

trines of grace". Those doctrines are dear to us as epitomising and concentrating the theology of the Bible, and as constituting, through the presence and power of the Christian Comforter, the spiritual life of our Churches.'[6]

To some extent we have anticipated ourselves, and overlapped the division that we made between 'conditional immortality' and 'the restitution of all things'. The doctrine of the ultimate salvation of all men was fervently propagated by Samuel Cox, a Nottingham Baptist minister, who was also and until 1884 the editor of 'The Expositor'. In that year the owners of the journal, Messrs. Hodder and Stoughton, determined on a change of editor because Cox had adopted the spreading heresy of the final salvation of all men, and also because of his views on the inspiration of Scripture were exceedingly lax. Cox set forth his ideas on the ultimate salvation of all men in *Salvator Mundi* which was first published in 1877. In the preface to the 1888 edition Cox could write: 'A remarkable change has passed over the mind of the Christian Church since this little book was published. And though I do not confound "post hoc" with "propter hoc" at least in this case I cannot but rejoice in the change, and venture to believe that I have taken a humble part in producing it. No one at all familiar with the religious life, or even with the pulpit of England can fail to have observed how largely the tone of thought on the future destiny of man has been modified during the last ten or twelve years.'[7] In the light of this statement it seems incredible that the council of the Baptist Union could deny during the Downgrade controversy that there had been any change in thought among Baptist ministers on the matter of eternal punishment.

Frequently allied with the doctrine of the restitution of all things is the idea of a period of remedial discipline after death for those who had died without faith in Christ. Cox, along with Canon F W Farrar whose book *Eternal Hope* was published in 1878, and others, taught this view which Spurgeon characterised as 'post-mortem salvation'.

Enough as been said in relation to eternal punishment to indicate how much the orthodox doctrine was being modified or altogether abandoned. We must turn now to the second area of doctrinal speculation and innovation. This concerned the doctrine of the atonement. In Calvinistic theology, as indeed in much Arminian theology, penal substitutionary atonement is basic. In the latter half of the

---

[6] *Ibid*
[7] *Op cit*, preface p vii–viii

nineteenth century, however, there was a rediscovery of the Greek fathers, and as a consequence the emphasis shifted from the atoning death of Christ to His incarnation. The incarnation was seen as the crown of a long process, and not as the remedy for a catastrophe. By some it was regarded as the atonement itself, the bringing together of God and man through Him who became man. It was the assumption of our flesh, rather than the bearing of our sins upon the Cross, that was of atoning value. Penal propitiatory and substitutionary atonement was branded as immoral and unnecessary, and not surprisingly the moral influence theory of the atonement became very popular. Spurgeon firmly opposed such teaching long before the Downgrade controversy disturbed the peace of the Baptist denomination. Perhaps the most striking statement he made against those who rejected substitutionary atonement was in a sermon preached before the Baptist Union Assembly at Leeds on October 16, 1878, on the text, 'We preach Christ crucified'. He dwelt upon the practical consequences of accommodating the Gospel to the thought of the age. 'We shall ask modern thought to bring its trophies; we shall ask the philosophers of the present period to bring up the those whom it has emancipated from sin. We will ask it to try its hand to commence evangelisation by teaching to man the wonderful theology, if it be advanced thought of modern culture. I think I see the harlots and sinners gathering together to listen to the talk. Yes, I think I see it once, but I am certain I should not see it twice ... '[8]

We have dwelt at length on the theological background to the Downgrade controversy in order to show that it is a part of a conflict in theology which was far wider in its compass than the Baptist denomination alone. The issues of eternal punishment and substitutionary atonement have received special attention since these doctrines were to be particularly prominent in the Downgrade controversy.

We have noticed how Spurgeon raised his voice as early as 1860 in protest against tendencies to heterodoxy in other denominations. Knowing the sort of man Spurgeon was, fearless and uncompromising when he considered Scriptural truth to be under attack, we shall not be surprised to find him protesting when these same tendencies manifested themselves in his own denomination.

---

[8] *The Christian World*, 1878, p 100, preserved in Spurgeon Scrapbooks, vol I

5.2   The Baptist Union

When the Baptist Union was founded in 1813 it was a voluntary association of Particular Baptist Churches. These Churches were Calvinistic in theology, and congregational in polity. The doctrinal basis of
the Union, though briefly stated, was emphatically Calvinistic: 'That
this society of ministers and Churches be designated "The General
Union of Baptist Ministers and Churches" maintaining the important doctrines of "three equal persons in the Godhead; eternal and
personal election; original sin; particular redemption; free justification by the imputed righteousness of Christ; efficacious grace in regeneration; the final perseverance of real believers; the resurrection
of the dead; the future judgement; the eternal happiness of the righ-
teous, and the eternal misery of such as die in impenitence, with the
congregational order of Churches inviolably".'[9]   In 1832, however,
the Union's constitution and basis was changed so as to permit the
entrance into it of Churches and ministers of the New Connexion of
General Baptists, which were Arminian in theology. The doctrinal
basis became simply agreement 'in the sentiments usually denomi-
nated evangelical'.

The acceptance of Churches of the New Connexion into the Baptist Union was only possible on a basis as vague as this. Any hint
of Calvinism in the doctrinal basis would have killed the chances of
gathering the Churches of the New Connexion into the Union. Yet
one is bound to ask whether a door was not opened in 1832 which
Spurgeon tried in vain to shut in 1887–8. In so far as Arminianism
allows a certain autonomy to man does it not inevitably lead to the
assertion of the principle of the autonomy of man's reason which is
the essence of 'modernism'?

In 1873 even the word 'evangelical' was dropped, much to the dis-
quiet of Spurgeon and others. Strangely enough it was a firm Calvinist, Charles Stovel, whose advocacy brought about this change. He
felt that believers' baptism by immersion provided a stronger doctrinal basis than evangelical sentiments. Spurgeon argued that it was
no time to be changing moorings, but he was over-ruled. A Declaration of Principle was adopted which declared that 'in this Union it is
fully recognised that every separate Church has liberty to interpret
and administer the laws of Christ, and that the immersion of believ-

---

[9]Quoted by E A Payne: *The Baptist Union — A Short History* (London, Carey
Kingsgate Press, 1959), p 24

ers is the only Christian baptism.'[10] It is clear that by this time the
Baptist Union had no real doctrinal basis, and consequently its constitution laid down no steps whereby ministers or churches guilty of
heresy could be removed from it. This became obvious to Spurgeon
in the course of the Downgrade controversy, and much of his energy
was devoted to an unsuccessful attempt to get the Union to adopt a
declaration of faith similar to the Evangelical Alliance.

The infiltration of the Baptists of the New Connexion into what
was originally a union of Particular Baptist Churches produced a
complex and confused ecclesiastical situation. Although the two denominations were not formally united until 1891, for all practical purposes they had merged long before. For example, in 1888 John Clifford, a General Baptist, was vice-president of the Baptist Union, and
as such played a large part in the Downgrade controversy, especially
since the president, Dr Culross, the President of Bristol Baptist College, lived out of London.

Undoubtedly as an instrument for co-operative enterprise the
Baptist Union was proving very useful. It aided poor pastors in country churches; it helped forward home mission work; it provided information. By 1887 it had become a unifying centre in a denomination of independent and autonomous Churches. As a writer in
the *Baptist Magazine* stated in November, 1878: 'The Baptist Union
has given to our denomination a cohesiveness which it did not before
possess.'[11] Spurgeon himself recognised the good work that the Baptist Union was doing in helping the strong churches to aid the weak.
He frequently appeared on the platform of the Union at the annual
assembly meetings up to 1883.

Spurgeon was one of the founder leaders of the London Baptist
Association which from 1865 onwards drew together both General
and Particular Baptist Churches in a harmonious fellowship. He was
especially active in promoting the building of Churches in the new
centres of population which were springing up in and around London.

The supreme body in the Baptist Union was the Council which
comprised the elected representatives of the Churches and associations. It was with this body of some one hundred members that Spurgeon was to deal, through his brother James, during the Downgrade
controversy. Spurgeon himself was never at any time a member of

---

[10] Quoted Payne, *op cit*, p 24
[11] *Baptist Magazine*, November 1878, preserved in Scrapbooks, I, p 110a

this body.

Continuity in administering the day to day affairs of the Union was provided by the secretary who, by this time, was a permanent paid official. He was to be a key figure in the Downgrade controversy. Samuel Harris Booth was secretary for two periods, from 1877–9, and from 1883–98. One of the significant omissions from every account of the controversy that I have read is a delineation of the personality and character of Booth. His theological outlook was similar to that of Spurgeon. Also, like Spurgeon, he upheld Puritan morality. He and Spurgeon were personal friends, and it appears that they consulted each other on denominational affairs quite freely. Dr Payne admits that 'There seems little doubt that in the mid eighteen-eighties they more than once discussed together the general denominational situation'.[12]

Booth's theological convictions were strong enough to cause him to protest at the preaching of W E Blomfield, the minister of the newly formed Church at Elm Road, Beckenham, of which Booth was a member. Blomfield's preaching, particularly what he omitted to say, left Booth doubtful about his orthodoxy. Tension developed between them, and although an enquiry by three denominational figures, J R Wood, E B Underhill and J W Todd, exonerated Blomfield, Booth and his wife withdrew from the church at Elm Road.

Despite this stand for orthodoxy, in the Downgrade controversy Booth was to vacillate, perhaps because he realised the strength of the feeling against Spurgeon. But in the years immediately preceding the outbreak of the controversy, Booth undoubtedly listened sympathetically to Spurgeon's expressions of concern over doctrinal deviation among certain ministers within the Baptist Union. Spurgeon's protest in 1887 was not, as is often assumed, unheralded. We have already noted his warning in a sermon preached before the annual assembly of the Union in 1878 of the perils of what he termed 'modern thought'.

From 1883 Spurgeon made active representations behind the scenes. His protests were originally occasioned by an incident which occurred at the Leicester assembly meetings of that year. A Unitarian minister, who had formerly been a Baptist pastor, at a mayoral reception made a number of flippant remarks, which gave considerable offence. Spurgeon was not present at this meeting, and he admitted that the Union officials could not be held responsible for what

---

[12]Payne, *op cit*, p 130

had happened. Evidently the incident made Spurgeon very uneasy, for he subsequently declined all invitations to preach for the Baptist Union and the Baptist Missionary Society. My own feeling is that the incident in itself is insufficient to account for Spurgeon's attitude, and that the explanation must lie in the circumstances which surrounded it. Perhaps it was the way in which certain persons received the Unitarian's remarks which most troubled Spurgeon. Whatever the reason for his attitude his policy is stated in a letter to the editor of the *Baptist* which is printed in Holden Pike's *Life of Spurgeon* (Vol VI, p 292). 'After a painful occurrence at Leicester, I made serious complaint to the secretary, to the president (Mr Chown), and others of the council. At the Orphanage, to which he kindly came, Mr Chown made to me a pathetic appeal to regard it as a solitary statement, and hoping that I had been mistaken, I did not go on with the matter, for which possibly I am blameworthy.'[13]

Spurgeon continues: 'Since then I have repeatedly spoken to the secretary upon the subject, as he will willingly admit. I think each year either himself or Mr Baynes had waited upon me to preach for the Union, or to preach at the Mission services connected with the Union gatherings. On each occasion one or other has heard my complaints till they must, I fear, have been wearied ... I have declined to take a public part in the meetings because I could not feel sure I would not be compromised thereby. This is surely an action which spoke more loudly than words ... I tried to compromise the matter with my judgement by joining in the work, and not the talk of the Union, and I wish it could have been a possible mid-way.'[14]

It has now become clear why Spurgeon was by 1887 a challenging figure on the edge of life of the Baptist Union. That in 1887 he should have raised his voice in public protest at doctrinal declension within the ranks should not have surprised those who were in the inner councils of the Union. That Spurgeon was made to appear by the officials and Council of the Union to have made sudden and unsubstantiated charges is a sad reflection upon their integrity.

---

[13] G Holden Pike: *The Life and Work of Charles Haddon Spurgeon* (London, Cassel & Co), vol VI, p 292

[14] *Ibid*, p 292

5.3   The Course of the Downgrade Controversy

In March and April 1887 two articles appeared in the Sword and
Trowel entitled 'The Downgrade'. They were by Robert Shindler,
who had been trained for the ministry at Spurgeon's own Pastors'
College, and currently the pastor of the Baptist Church at Addle-
stone, Surrey. The articles were both unsigned.

The first article dealt entirely with the defection of the eighteenth
century nonconformists from the standards of Calvinism. Spurgeon
drew attention to the timeliness of the article in an editorial foot-
note on its first page: 'Earnest attention is requested for this paper.
There is need of such a warning as this history affords. We are going downhill at break-neck speed.'[15] The identification of Calvinism
with evangelicalism was so complete that Spurgeon received letters
asking him if he considered the Wesleyan Methodists to be on the
Downgrade. In a note in the April issue Spurgeon declared that he
thought the Methodists were true to the great evangelical doctrines.
He made his own position clear: 'We care far more for the central
evangelical truths than we do for Calvinism as a system; but we believe that Calvinism has in it a conservative force which helps to hold
men to vital truth ... '[16] The real issue, to Spurgeon's mind, was not
Calvinism versus Arminianism: 'The present struggle is not a debate
upon the question of Calvinism or Arminianism, but of the truth of
God versus the inventions of men. All who believe the gospel should
unite against that "modern thought" which is its deadly enemy.'[17]

The second article by Shindler was even more Calvinistic in tone
that the first. Wesley is not even mentioned in his comments on the
Evangelical Revival, but Whitefield receives high praise. Again there
is no specific application to the present, except the implied warning that the errors of the eighteenth are in danger of being repeated
in the nineteenth century. Spurgeon added another editorial note:
'Again we call attention to this most important theme. The growing evil demands the attention of all who desire the prosperity of the
Church of God.'[18]

E B Underhill, a prominent member of the Baptist Union Council, said that he read the two articles with keen approval, but that he
had no idea that they were intended to apply in any way to the Bap-

---

[15] *Sword and Trowel*, March, 1887
[16] *Ibid*, p 195
[17] *Ibid*, p 196
[18] *Ibid*, p 196

tist denomination. This impression seems to have been general; they were too vague to indict directly any contemporary body of Christians.

When in the August issue of the *Sword and Trowel* Spurgeon entered the lists with an article entitled 'Another Word Concerning the Downgrade', the entire situation changed. The influence of Spurgeon was such that his views were bound to attract attention. In his article there was contemporary application in abundance. Spurgeon charged that 'A new religion has been initiated, which is no more Christianity than chalk is cheese; and this religion, being destitute of moral honesty, palms itself off as the old faith with slight improvements, and on this plea usurps pulpits which were erected for gospel preaching.'[19]

Spurgeon made two specific charges. First, that in many churches and chapels 'The Atonement is scouted, the inspiration of Scripture is derided, the Holy Spirit is degraded into an influence, the punishment of sin is turned into fiction, and the resurrection into a myth ...' The second charge was that 'At the back of doctrinal falsehood comes a natural decline of spiritual life, evidenced by a taste for questionable amusements, and a weariness of devotional meetings.'[20]

The article ended with some words on the practical question which now faced those who held to the old Gospel. 'It now becomes a serious question how far those who abide by the faith once delivered to the saints should fraternise with those who have turned aside to another gospel. Christian love has its claims, and divisions are to be shunned as grievous evils; but how far are we justified in being in confederacy with those who are departing from the truth?'[21]

The following month Spurgeon published another article, 'Our Reply to Sundry Critics and Enquirers'. In this he dealt mainly with those persons who pressed him for names and facts to support his assertion that the Churches were on the Downgrade. His reply was simple. 'Had there been a right spirit in those who resent our warning, they would either have disproved our charge, or else they would have lamented its truthfulness, and have set to work to correct the evil which we lamented.'[22]

A third article from Spurgeon's pen appeared in the October issue of his magazine. It was entitled 'The Case Proved'. After deal-

---

[19] *Ibid*, p 397
[20] *Ibid*, p 397
[21] *Ibid*, p 400
[22] *Ibid*, p 463

ing with the various objections which had been brought against his protest Spurgeon shows that he feels that there is little chance of convincing his opponents by giving them masses of detail to support his case. He wrote that 'Those who have made up their minds to ignore the gravity of the crisis would not be aroused from their composure though we told our tale in miles of mournful detail.'[23] Spurgeon concluded the article with these solemn words: 'What action is to be taken we leave to those who can see more plainly than we do what Israel ought to do. One thing is clear to us — we cannot be expected to meet in any union which comprehends those whose teaching is, upon fundamental points, exactly the reverse of that which we hold dear ... With deep regret we abstain from assembling with those whom we dearly love and heartily respect, since it would involve us in a confederacy with those with whom we have no communion in the Lord.'[24]

Immediately after the publication of the last of the Downgrade articles the Baptist Union autumn meetings were held in Sheffield. No formal notice was taken of the articles, but Spurgeon seems to have expected that the charges he had made would have been discussed. Doubtless the Council of the Union ignored Spurgeon's protests out of a sincere desire to maintain peace. However, at a public meeting two speakers made caustic remarks about Spurgeon's charges, to which no reply could then be made. The situation was not improved when the 'The Freeman' published, on 14th October, 1887, a facetious paragraph which said that in the train on the way to Sheffield 'the great joke was the Downgrade question'. Though apology was later made for this statement, it seriously wounded Spurgeon and some of his friends.

On October 28, 1887, Spurgeon wrote to Dr Booth to intimate his withdrawal from the Baptist Union. 'I do this,' he wrote, 'with the utmost regret, but I have no choice. The reasons are set forth in *Sword and Trowel* for November, and I trust you will excuse my repeating them here. I beg you not to send anyone to me to ask for reconsideration. I fear I have considered too long already. Certainly every hour of the day impresses upon me the conviction that I am moving none too soon.[25]

Various attempts to heal the breach were made, but all in vain. Spurgeon was visited by a deputation from the Union which urged

[23] *Ibid*, p 514
[24] *Ibid*, p 514
[25] Quoted J J Ellis: *Charles Haddon Spurgeon* (London, Nisbet & Co) p 169

him to reconsider his decision to withdraw. Spurgeon urged upon its members the necessity of a credal basis similar, he suggested, to that of the Evangelical Alliance. However, he viewed his attempt to get the Union on a proper credal basis as a last ditch measure, for he had not much faith in creeds, and had often told his students so. The reason for his lack of confidence was the knowledge he had that some men are base enough to deny the truths which subscription to a confession of faith binds them to preach.

Nevertheless, as the Downgrade controversy progressed Spurgeon seems to have changed his position somewhat. In answering those who objected to any creed whatsoever Spurgeon replied: 'Surely, what we believe may be stated, may be written, may be made known; and what is this but to make and promulgate a creed? Baptists from the first have issued their confessions of faith. Even the present Baptist Union has a creed about baptism, though about nothing else.'[26] 'To say,' argued Spurgeon, 'that "a creed comes between a man and his God", it to suppose that it is not true, for truth, however definitely stated, does not divide the believer from his Lord.' He made a telling point, later to be elaborated so forcibly by Gresham Machen in his 'Christianity and Liberalism: 'I am unable to sympathise with a man who says he has no creed; because I believe him to be in the wrong by his own showing. He ought to have a creed. What is equally certain, he has a creed — he must have one, even though he repudiates the notion. His very unbelief is, in a sense, a creed.'[27]

In an attempt to meet Spurgeon's wishes, Dr Joseph Angus, the principal of Regent's Park College, drew up a declaration of belief with Spurgeon's brother, James. Despite some determined opposition this was accepted by the Council at a meeting on February 21st, 1888, to be presented to the Assembly in April. Many thought that this declaration would provide a basis for reunion. James Spurgeon was among them, for at the Assembly he seconded the motion in favour of its adoption. It was accepted by an overwhelming vote, 2,000 to 7 against.

Yet to the central figure in the controversy it was not acceptable because apart from what Spurgeon called its omissions on the crucial issue of eternal punishment there was equivocation. A historical note was added to the section on the Resurrection and the Judgment at the Last Day, 'according to the words of our Lord in Matthew 25:46'

---

[26] *Sword and Trowel*, 1888, p 82
[27] *Ibid*, p 82

which declared: 'It should be stated as an historical fact, that there have been brethren in the Union, working cordially with it, who while reverently bowing to the authority of Holy Scripture, and rejecting the dogmas of Purgatory and Universalism, have not held the common interpretation of the words of our Lord'.[28] By this stratagem, as Spurgeon clearly saw, the door was left open for those who maintained conditional immortality and annihilation. And it ought not to pass unnoticed that exactly the same stratagem was employed at the November, 1971 Council meeting of the Baptist Union which, on the one hand reaffirmed the declaration of principle including the phrase that our Lord is 'God manifest in the flesh', and on the other hand, permitted the passing of an addendum which clearly sanctions liberty to deny the deity of Christ. History has a strange way of repeating itself!

Spurgeon, throughout the controversy, refused to deal in personalities or to give names of those whom he suspected of heresy. Because of this he was criticised for making a 'charge against anonymity'. Tactically his opponents scored a fine debating point which weighed heavily with many people. But he refused to name names because 'he did not believe that the Union had any authority over them, nor did he know of anyone who had violated the Constitution, because he did not believe there is any power under our Constitution for dealing with the utmost divergence of doctrinal opinion'.[29] Spurgeon thus pressed first for a credal basis, and was only prepared to talk of discipline when this had been adopted. In his view the Baptist Union had only one article in its basis — believers' baptism by immersion — and this was totally inadequate. 'To form a union with a single Scriptural ordinance as its sole distinctive reason for existence has been well likened to erecting a pyramid upon its apex; the whole edifice must sooner or later come down'.[30] As Spurgeon pointed out on such a basis 'No one can be heterodox under this constitution unless he should forswear his baptism. I offered to pay fee for Counsel's opinion on this matter, but my offer was not accepted ... Whatever may be said to the contrary, if we go to the authorised declaration of principles it is clear that the Union is incompetent for any doctrinal judgment, except it should be needful to ascertain a person's views on baptism. I decline to submit to it any case that would be quite

---

[28]Quoted Payne, *op cit,* p 140
[29]Minute of the meeting on 13th January, 1888, between Cilross, Clifford, Booth and Spurgeon at the Metropolitan Tabernacle, quoted Payne *op cit,* pp 135–6
[30]*Sword and Trowel,* 1888, p 83

beyond its powers.'[31]

Holding this view of the nature of the Union, Spurgeon's indignation at the Council's 'Vote of Censure' passed on January 18th, 1888, is readily understandable. The motion stated, 'That the Council recognises the gravity of the charges which Mr Spurgeon has brought against the Union previous to and since his withdrawal. It considers the public and general manner in which they have been made reflects upon the whole body, and exposes to suspicion brethren who love the truth as dearly as he does. And, as Mr Spurgeon declined to give the names of those to whom he intended them to apply, and the evidence supporting them, those charges, in the judgment of the Council, ought never to have been made.'[32] Willis Glover, who certainly does not sympathise with Spurgeon's doctrine, describes the resolution as 'a political manœuvre',[33] and so it was. Clifford, Alexander Maclaren and Charles Williams had rejected the inerrancy of the Scriptures, and yet they voted as they did when they knew that Spurgeon's charges at that particular point applied to themselves. Clifford, during the last two years of his life seems to have felt much anxiety over the Council's treatment of Spurgeon, and his own part in it.[34]

Other developments in the course of the controversy need not long detain us. Because Spurgeon had evidence that some of the men trained in his own College had become unorthodox, he re-organised the College Conference which hitherto every graduate of the College had a right to attend. The old Conference was dissolved and a new one formed with a clear declaration of faith as the basis for association. This remained unaltered until 1961. Of the 496 members of the former Conference, 432 agreed to the new basis and were formed into the Pastors' College Evangelical Association. The College remained outside of the Baptist Union until 1938, the Metropolitan Tabernacle until 1955, but it again withdrew in 1971.

On Tuesday, 11th April 1888, Spurgeon withdrew from the London Baptist Association which he had helped to form in 1865. In an unpublished letter to a former student of the Pastors' College dated June 16 1888, Spurgeon made clear his position in relation to the London Baptist Association. 'Are you in the Association? If so, you will still be in the Union. The Surrey, Middlesex and Suburban is

---

[31] *Irish Baptist Magazine*, 1888, p 28
[32] Quoted Payne, *op cit*, p 136
[33] *Op cit*, p 173
[34] Sir James Marchant: *Dr John Clifford*, (London), p 161

quitting the Union, and I shall probably unite with it. This will be an Association outside the Union, sound in doctrine, and thus the nucleus of a fresh Union should the time come.'[35] Spurgeon did in fact join this Association of churches, which was renamed the Home Counties Association.

5.4   The Main Issues

There were two main issues in the Downgrade controversy, the second flowing from the former. The first was doctrinal, the second ecclesiastical.

The doctrinal issue was this. Spurgeon believed that there was one Gospel, the same in every age, the faith once for all delivered to the saints. In particular Spurgeon attacked those who minimised the atonement and who abandoned the doctrine of eternal punishment. The inspiration of Scripture, and the actual bodily resurrection of our Lord were also issues, but they did not figure so prominently in the controversy as the other matters. Spurgeon took the stand he did, come wind, come weather, because he utterly repudiated the notion of an undoctrinal Christianity based upon sentiment. He did not, and could not, accept the view that evangelicalism is but a point of view among other equally valid theological options. He believed that the doctrines of grace were truth itself, to be accepted as the revelation of the living God in a humble submission of mind and heart.

The second main issue, the ecclesiastical, was a corollary of the first. What sort of union would the Baptist Union be? Should it be a union of churches based only on believers' baptism by immersion, or a union founded upon the fundamental truth of Holy Scripture? Was the Union to be, in Spurgeon's words, 'like Noah's ark, afford(ing) shelter both for the clean and unclean, for creeping things and winged fowls?'[36] Or was it to be 'an avowedly Evangelical body on the old lines of faith?'[37] Spurgeon dogmatically declared for a union of churches based upon Scriptural doctrine. For him no other principle of association was adequate.

In a key passage in his account of the Downgrade controversy, A C Underwood writing in 1947 pinpoints the issue: 'After more than fifty years, few, if any Baptists are now other than thankful the Union

---

[35] A copy of this letter is in the author's possession
[36] *Sword and Trowel,* 1888, p 82
[37] *ibid,* p 83

took the stand it did and refused Spurgeon's demand that it should accept a definite creed in place of its Declaration of Faith'.[38] One readily understands why in such a union a man may now blatantly deny the deity of Christ and yet cannot be disciplined, for without a proper confessional basis he has as much right to be there as the most fervent upholder of our Lord's deity. Yet the present situation in the Baptist Union is not different 'in principle' from what it was at the time of the Downgrade and has been ever since. The only difference is that heresy has reached its ultimate point — the denial of the deity of our Lord.

Spurgeon did not take the fashionable line of today —'Don't let us bother about the doctrine, let us get on with evangelism' — because he saw the practical consequences which would follow from departure from the doctrines of grace. He believed that there could be no hope for the sinner in the new theology, nor any holiness for the saint. He declared it would empty churches, not fill them. 'Assuredly the New Theology can do no good toward God or man; it has no adaption for it. If it were preached for a thousand years by all the most earnest men of the school, it would never renew a soul, nor overcome pride in a single human heart.'[39] In 1888 he wrote: 'Those who do away with Christian doctrine are, whether they are aware of it or not, the worst enemies of Christian living. The godliness of Puritanism will not long survive the sound doctrine of Puritanism. The coals of orthodoxy are necessary to the fire of piety'.[40]

Spurgeon was undoubtedly right in his insight into the religious situation of his time. He saw the marks of death where others could only see signs of health. He saw that churches would become worldly and powerless in proportion as they departed from the truth. He realised that a decline in vital godliness would be produced by a departure from those doctrines which are productive of godliness — the depravity of the sinner, the atoning, propitiatory sacrifice of Christ, the absolute necessity of regeneration and the sanctifying work of the Holy Spirit.

I close this section of my paper with a story concerning W L Watkinson, a great Methodist preacher of three generations ago. In a conversation with the Rev John Thomas a few days before he died, Watkinson said: 'There is one other word concerning Spurgeon I can-

---

[38] A C Underwood: *A History of English Baptists*, (London, Carey Kingsgate Press, 1947), p 230

[39] *Sword and Trowel*, 1887, preface, p iii

[40] *Sword and Trowel*, 1888, p 62

not omit'. We spoke of his mighty protest in the early days of the apostasy, and Dr Watkinson said: 'In days gone by there was a saying among the North American Indians in which they said of a man who was keen of discernment and quick to detect dangers, "He hears the cataract".' Then turning to me, he said in his most inimitable and dramatic manner, 'Charles Haddon Spurgeon heard the cataract'.[41]

5.5   Some Relevant Conclusions

1. Spurgeon found that many ministers and laymen who claimed they were evangelical were unwilling to define the content of the evangelical faith. Their successors are with us to-day, just as protestingly evangelical and just as unwilling to say what they mean by the word. Spurgeon proved that in the heat of conflict such men will be found wanting to-day.

2. The Downgrade controversy is a classic illustration of the bewitching power of denominationalism. Spurgeon's protest was largely in vain because good men's eyes were blinded by the necessity (as they saw it) of preserving the peace and unity of the Baptist Union. Staunch evangelicals cried 'peace' when Spurgeon lifted up his voice because they could not, or would not, see that sometimes peace is disturbed by truth.

3. Spurgeon knew that when all the speculations of men fall into the dust to which they belong, the Gospel of free grace would shine forth in yet greater splendour because it is God-originated and God-owned. He said that he was willing to be eaten of dogs for the next fifty years, but the more distant future would vindicate him. He prophesied that there would be a return to the doctrines of grace because he knew that the waters of life were not to be found in the wells of the new theology.

To-day I believe that his words are coming true — we are beginning to see a movement back to the doctrines of grace. May God grant us all to feel the power of these precious truths in our hearts, give us grace to adorn the doctrine we profess and above all visit us with a heaven-sent revival which will do more to vindicate the truths for which Spurgeon stood than anything else.

---

[41]Pamphlet on centenary of Spurgeon's birth, published by the Protestant Truth Society, 1934

5.6   1992 Postscript

Since the paper which forms this chapter was first presented in 1971, two significant developments have taken place. First, there has been a steady if unspectacular growth, largely but not exclusively in the English-speaking world, in the number of churches which adhere to the 1689 Baptist Confession of Faith.

This confession was reprinted by C H Spurgeon in 1855 and it can be said to represent his convictions in matters doctrinal and ecclesiastical. That the distinctive Calvinistic doctrines of the Confession are of continuing relevance and interest is witnessed by the fact that in recent years it has been translated into several languages including Russian, Romanian, Hungarian, French, Spanish, Zulu and Afrikaans both as a basis for association between churches, an instrument for reformation, and a means of instruction. The 1689 Confession, neglected for generations, is now proving its enduring worth. It can, therefore, with some justice be said that the system of doctrine for which Spurgeon stood, and which attracted such obloquy during the Downgrade controversy, is now enjoying an increasingly pervasive revival. The republication of Spurgeon's sermons and many of his other works is also a contributing factor.[42] As no other notable preacher of the nineteenth century, Spurgeon speaks today as we near the end of the twentieth century.

A second and ironical development has been the growth of annihilationism in the last twenty years or so. Once largely a closet belief (both Basil Atkinson's and H E Guillebaud's books were published posthumously) annihilationism against which Spurgeon argued so strongly, is now openly espoused by an increasing number of evangelical ministers, especially those belonging to the evangelical wing of the Church of England. Both John Stott[43] and Philip Edgcumbe Hughes[44] have declared themselves in favour of it though both have been firmly answered by James Packer.[45]

It is ironical that annihilationism is now being viewed as an acceptable (and some would maintain, equally biblical) alternative to the traditional belief in the doctrine of everlasting punishment. For Spurgeon it was not, and could not be an alternative. It was rather

---

[42] By Pilgrim Publishers, Pasadena, Texas

[43] Stott, *Essentials* (with David Edwards)

[44] Philip Edgcumbe Hughes, *The True Image*, Eerdmans, 1989

[45] J I Packer, in *Evangelical Affirmations*, edd. Kenneth S Kantzer and Carl F H Henry, p 113ff, Zondervan USA

an unbiblical heresy which to his mind threatened the very mission of the church.

Whether annihilationism will continue to grow within evangelical circles remains to be seen. One thing is certain, Spurgeon would never have countenanced the idea that evangelicalism can be redefined so as to include annihilationism within its compass. At the risk of being labelled sectarian, were he alive today, he would have denounced it as vigorously as he denounced it before and during the Downgrade controversy.

Chapter 6

Spurgeon's Politics

It is said that in the 1880s an American Sunday-school child was asked, 'Who is the Prime Minister of England?' The boy replied, 'Mr Spurgeon!' If this anecdote is apocryphal it nevertheless accurately reflects the worldwide influence of C H Spurgeon and his prominence in the political sphere. It may also indicate comparative ignorance (at least in America) of the real Prime Minister, Mr Gladstone, whose periods in office spanned the years 1868–94. Whether in office or out of office, it was Gladstone who commanded the support and loyalty of the British nonconformist churches and their leaders — most of the time. Spurgeon himself was an ardent champion of Gladstone's brand of Liberalism; he also had great personal admiration and affection towards Gladstone the man, and this was reciprocated. The two men, who operated on different wavelengths as far as ecclesiastical matters were concerned, were on exactly the same frequency when it came to public morality and indeed personal spirituality. This affinity played an important part in the Nonconformists' electoral support for the Liberal party.

Spurgeon was not one who subscribed to the notion held by some that Christians, and especially ministers, ought to remain aloof from the grubby world of politics. He was convinced, on the contrary, that the political sphere lay within the 'world' to which Christians were called to be an influence for good: 'It is not for the Christian', he wrote in 1879, 'to descend into the dirt and treachery of politics, but ... to draw politics up into the light and power of Christ ... The United States has shown us what horrible corruption is engendered by Christian men refusing to be the salt and light of the world; let it not be so among us.'[1] 'Every God-fearing man', he wrote in another place, 'should give his vote with as much devotion as he prays.' From the pulpit Spurgeon was careful not to 'sink the spiritual in the temporal', but, as we shall see, he had no qualms in expressing political opinions and even exerting political pressure outside the pulpit.

Before examining in detail Spurgeon's political involvement and drawing important conclusions, we need to form a clear idea of the religious and political context of the Victorian England in which Spurgeon operated. In doing so, we will take a closer look at the figure of Gladstone and at Spurgeon's relationship with him.

The Victorian age was one of incredible progress in many areas of the nation's life — democratic government, social improvement, industrial development, imperial expansion — but it witnessed a significant decline in evangelical religion. In the early part of the century it was evangelicalism that had been the main impulse in both Anglicanism and Nonconformity: by the end of the nineteenth century it had almost died out. Modernism and Higher Criticism took such a hold in the Nonconformist denominations that they lost confidence in the Biblical gospel. The Calvinism of the Puritans and the revival preachers in the previous two centuries, though fanned into flame by Spurgeon, was only smoldering embers as the twentieth century dawned. Spurgeon fought a rearguard action in the 'Downgrade Controversy' in 1887, but to no avail. Evangelical influence within the Church of England was at its height in the first half of the century. In 1853 a quarter of all the clergy were evangelical, mainly thanks to the labours of Charles Simeon at Cambridge. As the century progressed, however, the Oxford, or Tractarian Movement, which had begun in the 1830s, spread a ritualistic, authoritarian emphasis in an effort to restate Anglican identity in the light of perceived threats to its privileges and status. Some of the clergy seceded to Rome; many stayed in the Church of England as Anglo-Catholics.

Nevertheless the Britain in which Spurgeon came to prominence was a society which still bore the imprint of the mighty acts of God in the Great Awakening and as recently as the 1859 revival. The Victorian conscience reached a high degree of moral sensitivity; moral energy flowing from this gave the impetus to much-needed social reforms. Evangelical Christianity had permeated the national character to such an extent that it shaped the public's expectations of their

---

[1] *Sword and Trowel*, bound volume for 1879, p 41. (All volumes of this magazine can be seen in the Evangelical Library, 78A Chiltern Street, London W1)

politicians. In 1876 the 'Spectator' commented, in relation to the 'Bulgarian Atrocities' protest:

'... the moral feelings of the country have been gathering purity and force from the growing interest in those religious strifes which take little account of political expediency, and make inconveniently sharp distinctions between right and wrong. ... Thus a large part of the nation has been silently, slowly and unconsciously learning to apply more rigorous moral tests to political actions ...'.

It is not too much to say that in Britain, uniquely among the nations of the world, the foremost criterion by which the people judged the actions of their government was a moral one, and that this was because the nation's conscience was evangelically-informed.

Thus, despite the general picture of decline in evangelism, its force sharpened the nation's moral senses. The declining stream still irrigated the land. When in the 1890s an issue equally as momentous as the 'Bulgarian Atrocities' came before the public, it was greeted not with organised protest and moral indignation, but indifference and apathy. By this time the stream had run dry.

The alliance between Nonconformity and the Liberal party is perhaps the most striking feature of British political history between the late 1860s and the mid 1880s. The Nonconformists regarded Gladstone as 'the incarnation of the highest ideal of political morality'. What accounts for the alliance? The Nonconformists were aggrieved at the political, religious and educational disabilities imposed on them by the Anglican Establishment and lifted only gradually during the nineteenth century. Had Spurgeon felt the need to study for a degree at Oxford or Cambridge, as a Dissenter he could not have done so. No Dissenter could hold public office until 1828 when the Test and Corporation act was repealed — in practice, however, it was not until Gladstone's first administration in 1868–74 that Dissenters were included in the Cabinet. But it was the religious handicaps which most galled the Nonconformists. They were liable for church rates, even though, according to the census of 1851, the Church of England only enjoyed a marginal numerical superiority over the Dissenters. They were obliged to be married in the parish church but could not be buried in its churchyard. These disabilities were more pronounced, and more resented, in country areas than in the towns. Thus Spurgeon when he came to London in 1854 brought with him a healthy dislike both for the Church of England and the Tory party which upheld and defended it. It was only natural that the Nonconformists should look to the Liberals, 'the party of progress', to further their cause. Spurgeon's personal attachment to Gladstone was at the core of his loyalty to the Liberal party: his own political creed matched that of Gladstone — 'Peace, Retrenchment, Reform.' It is worth examining the man who was Spurgeon's 'honoured chief'.

William Ewart Gladstone was born in Liverpool in 1809, the year of Abraham Lincoln's birth. He was of Scottish descent. His father was a prosperous merchant and his mother, who exerted a profound influence during William's childhood, was an evangelical believer. In later life Gladstone recalled being taken by his parents as a boy of six to seek the advice of 'Mr Simeon' at Cambridge as to a vicar for a church near Liverpool of which his father was the benefactor. Gladstone was educated at Eton and Christ Church, Oxford, from where he graduated with a double first in Classics and Mathematics. He entered Parliament as a Tory in 1833 and rose rapidly up the political ladder. Siding with Peel over the repeal of the Corn Laws in 1846, he eventually identified with the emerging Liberal party and demonstrated such ability that he became the obvious choice for leader after the demise of Palmerston in 1865.

He was Prime Minister for a total of nearly 13 years in four different spells of office between 1868 and 1894. Gladstone's achievements were far-reaching. At the Board of Trade in the 1840s he oversaw the railway boom and was responsible for regulating the companies which ran them. He brought in the London Docks Act, which greatly improved the miserable working conditions of the London dockers. In the 1850s and early 1860s as Chancellor of the Exchequer he pursued classical Liberal 'laissez faire' economic policies, reducing taxes and tariffs on imported goods, reducing public spending and bringing 'moral enfranchisement' to millions of ordinary people by the repeal of the Paper Duty, which brought books, pamphlets and newspapers within their price range for the first time. His government of 1868–74 achieved 'the day's work of a giant' — vital reforms were carried through in many areas of national life, often in the teeth of Establishment opposition. In the army, flogging during peace time was finally abolished and the privilege of buying a commission was ended. The English judicial system was considerably simplified by the Judicature Act of 1872. Religious tests for entry to the universities were withdrawn. The Education Act of 1870 paved the way for a national system of compulsory education. The right to strike was granted to the trades unions in 1871. In the following year the Ballot Act made voting secret for the first time. All the major branches of the Civil Service, except the Foreign Office, were opened up to competitive examination. Gladstone fulfilled his election pledge to reduce public expenditure from the high level at which the previous Tory administration had left it: in 1873 the country was spending no more than in 1868, and during those years nearly £30 million of debt was paid off.

Gladstone was a man of prodigious mental and physical energy, of high principle and profound conviction. He was also extremely complicated and not as outwardly appealing as the more straightforward Spurgeon. His primary motive was the sense of calling to carry out God's purposes in politics. For him every issue, great or small, had a moral dimension. Two things in particular were abhorrent to him — war and waste. 'The expenses of war,' he wrote, 'are a moral check which it has pleased the Almighty to impose upon the ambition and lust for conquest that are inherent in so many nations.' He had an acute sense of accountability to God right from the outset of his adult life. As he embarked on his career in politics he wrote to his father that he was '... a being destined shortly to stand before the judgment seat of God and there give the decisive account of his actions.' All experiences in public life he related his own sanctification. He had a seemingly endless capacity for self-examination and his formidable critical faculties constantly sifted his own motives and desires. He confides in his diary[2] in 1841:

> 'O depth and mystery of the heart of man, who can fathom it or tell whether his acts of seeming duty, his inward moments of penitence and love, are really genuine single energies of spiritual life or are the mechanism of hypocrisy intended to deceive the Lord his judge but deceiving himself alone?'

Then in 1843 in more positive vein:

> 'O mystery impenetrable of the soul of man! Who is sufficient for these things, save only the promises of

---

[2]The Gladstone Diaries are a thorough record of Gladstone's daily life for more than seventy years. They are half as long again as the Bible! Mostly the diary is strictly information as to books read, letters written, meetings attended and people spoken to. but occasionally, most often on his birthday (December 29th) he reflects on the course of his public and private life. These glimpses are especially fascinating and show Gladstone to be sincere and rigorously self-critical, not at all the archetypal Victorian hypocrite portrayed by critics earlier this century. He called his diary 'an account-book of the all precious gift of Time'. It was never intended to be published. But the documents were made available and in 1968 the Oxford University Press began to publish 'The Gladstone Diaries'. The task continues today!

Christ ... May the washing of His blood be upon the past
and the renewing and indwelling power of His Spirit in
the future.'

Reflecting in later life he wrote, 'Two things are ever before me,
clear and unchanging: the unbounded goodness of God, and my
deep, deep, deep unworthiness."

Gladstone's inner life seems to have been thoroughly evangelical, and his statements on most of the major doctrines, e.g. the inspiration and infallibility of the Scriptures, the substitutionary atoning work of Christ, and the eternal punishment of the wicked, are
orthodox. Yet Gladstone was not an Evangelical. He was a High
Church Anglican all his days. He held to baptismal regeneration. He
was hopelessly ecumenical, viewing the Church of England as being
'... in the centre of all the conflicting forms of Christianity.' He clung
to the vision that '... in substance the movement termed Evangelical
and that falsely termed Popish are parts of the one great and benef-
icent design of God, and ... in their substance they will harmonize
and cooperate.' He firmly espoused the concept of national religion
and held that the State's duty was to support the Church of England
and tolerate the others. Near the end of his life, however, he seemed
to repudiate this idea: '... the State has no charter from heaven', he
wrote in 1894, 'such as may belong to the Church or to the individual
conscience. It would, as I think, be better for the State to limit itself
to giving secular instruction (which of course is not complete education).' Having said all this, we should bear in mind the comment
of one biographer that Gladstone '... pottered at theology all his life
but rarely understood the nature of any great theological question
he ever handled.'

Spurgeon got on with Gladstone much better than their differences in age (Gladstone was 25 years older), temperament and ecclesiology would suggest. He wrote to Gladstone on 16th April 1869:

> 'As one among thousands I have watched your career
> with an almost affectionate admiration; not only because
> for the most part I have agreed with your politics, but
> because I have seen in you a man actuated by a sense of
> right, in contradistinction to the pitiful shifts of policy.'

In the matter of disestablishing the Church of Ireland Spurgeon
assured Gladstone of the Dissenters' support and '... the devout
prayers of those to whom it is a matter of solemn conscience that

our Lord's kingdom is not of this world. We see in you', he continued, 'an answer to many a fervent petition that the day may come
when the Church of Jesus may believe in her Lord's power and not
in human alliances.' Spurgeon closed the letter humbly in this way:

> 'I do not expect even a line from your secretary to
> acknowledge this. It will content me for once in my life to
> have said "Thank-you" and "God-speed" to such a man.
> Yours very respectfully, C H Spurgeon.'

Gladstone in turn greatly admired Spurgeon, especially for his
preaching with its testimony 'of sin, of righteousness and of judgment: and its great earnestness and power.' At the beginning of 1882
Gladstone, then in his second spell as Prime Minister, wrote to Spurgeon asking for a seat to be reserved for him at the Tabernacle for
the forthcoming Sunday evening service. Spurgeon replied:

> 'I feel like a boy who is to preach with his father to
> listen to him. I shall try not to know that you are there at
> all, but just preach to my poor people the simple word
> which has held them in their thousands these twenty-
> eight years. You do not know how those of us regard
> you who feel it is a joy to live when a Premier believes in
> righteousness. We believe in no man's infallibility, but it
> is restful to be sure of one man's integrity.'

Thus on January 8th 1882 Gladstone with his son William attended the Metropolitan Tabernacle. They met Spurgeon in the
vestry and came out onto the platform with him and the elders and
deacons. Spurgeon preached on 'The Touch' from Mark 5:30. Gladstone recorded in his diary: 'In the Evening went with Willy to Mr
Spurgeon's Tabernacle. Saw him before & after. There would be
much to say upon it ... ' Presumably good, since Gladstone had expressed his delight after the service. Gladstone got into some trouble
for visiting the Tabernacle. But one correspondent wrote:
'The visit of the most intellectual of the High Church laymen to
the most conspicuous Nonconformist chapel in England is an event
of historic interest. Two great moral personalities, the Premier and
Mr Spurgeon, have accidentally fraternised within a dissenting en-
closure ... Why shouldn't Gladstone go and hear Spurgeon? The

Tabernacle Pastor has turned Calvinism into poetry ... He has made a morose faith musical.'[3]

The two men rarely had a chance to meet and talk. For reasons either of illness or pressure of work Spurgeon was unable to accept several invitations from Gladstone either to Downing Street or to Hawarden, his country home near Chester. They did meet once at Downing Street: on this occasion Gladstone pressed Spurgeon to stay on after the ten minutes allotted had run out. At Spurgeon's 50th birthday celebrations at the Tabernacle in 1884, a tribute arrived by telegram from Mr Gladstone. Spurgeon said that it meant more to him than all the others. In his final illness the depth of the bond between the two men is evident. Gladstone wrote to Mrs Spurgeon:

'In my own home, darkened at the present time, I have read with sad interest the daily accounts of Mr Spurgeon's illness; and I cannot help conveying to you the earnest assurance of my sympathy with you and with him, and of my cordial admiration, not only of his splendid powers, but still more of his devoted and unfailing character. May I humbly commend you and him, in all contingencies, to the infinite stores of the Divine love and mercy.'

Mrs Spurgeon wrote back and Spurgeon was well enough to add his own postscript: 'Yours is a word of love such as those only who write who have been into the King's country and have seen much of His face. My heart's love to you — C H Spurgeon.'[4]

Once Spurgeon achieved the pre-eminence as the most famous preacher in the land, he was consulted for his opinion on almost every issue of public concern. He became well-known as a Liberal supporter and it was not always easy for the public to draw a line between his role as pastor of the Tabernacle congregation and as a leading political Dissenter. Spurgeon was careful about letting the Tabernacle to political associations or pressure groups, but he was happy for its use by the Liberation Society, a pressure group seeking the disestablishment of the Church of England. Spurgeon was wholeheartedly behind this, but had to dissociate himself from the Society in 1891 when 'Freethinkers' began to become prominent within its ranks. 'We will not', he wrote, '... be brought into apparent union with those from whom we differ in the very core of our souls upon matters vital to Christianity.'

---

[3] Quoted in *Spurgeon and his friendships* by A Cunningham-Burley, Epworth Press, 1933, p 126

[4] Quoted in *The Life of Charles Haddon Spurgeon* by Charles Ray, (Passmore & Alabaster, 1903), p 389

Clearly Spurgeon's political involvement was never at the expense of the interests of the faith. But there were some political issues which, in Spurgeon's mind, rose above others and on which he felt bound to speak. In 1884 he declared:

> 'Whenever topics touch the rights of man, righteousness, peace, and so on, come in my way, I endeavour to speak as emphatically as I can on the right side. It is a part of my religion to desire justice and freedom for all.'

In the General Election of 1868, taking up the cause of the Irish Disestablishment, Spurgeon urged Dissenters to be:

> '... looking out for Dissenting representatives to send up to the next parliament ... We must disendow the Irish Church, and abolish Church rates at once, and to do this there ought to be a strong Nonconformist element in the House. Truth and righteousness demand of Christian electors that they should bestir themselves.'[5]

The case against an established church was made by Spurgeon's example as well as his words. Patricia Kruppa[6] writes of Spurgeon in 1869:

> '... he was the most popular preacher in the country, pastor of the largest independent congregation in the world, and director of a diversified philanthropic organisation. Everything he had accomplished he owed to his talents and the contributions of his followers. The state gave him no rates, no living, no cathedral. None of his institutions were subsidized by the state, yet all flourished ... Churchmen grew weary of refuting his example ... Bishop Wilberforce, asked if he did not envy the Nonconformists their Spurgeon, replied, 'It is written, "Thou shalt not covet thy neighbour's ass."' '

Spurgeon's energetic opposition to the Church of England would not be appeased merely by reforming it — it would have to go! When

---

[5] *Sword and Trowel*, March 1868

[6] Patricia Stallings Kruppa (Professor of History at the University of Texas in Austin), *C H Spurgeon: A Preacher's Progress* (Garland, 1982); chapter VI, 'A Political Dissenter'. This chapter is a mine of information on Spurgeon's politics.

Bishop Wilberforce played down the differences between Nonconformists and Anglicans, Spurgeon nearly exploded. 'Does he really
believe', he wrote in *Sword and Trowel*, 'that there is no necessity
for Dissent from a church which has now become so like to the anti-
Christ of Rome that if a hue and cry were raised for Babylon's twin
sister, she would certainly be arrested?'[7] It was Spurgeon's hope that
Irish disestablishment was just the beginning of a programme of systematic eradication of Church-State links: 'Therefore laying the axe
at the root of the system, we demand the abolition of every union between church and state, and the disallowance on the part of Cæsar
with things which belong to God.'[8] The overwhelming Liberal victory in the General Election of December 1868 — the party gained a
majority of 112 seats in the House of Commons — thrilled Spurgeon
and all the Nonconformists, Irish Disestablishment soon became law
and still greater things were hoped for. One of the biggest issues
in the Liberal reform programme to excite Nonconformist attention
was education. For Spurgeon, and for Dissenters generally, the voluntary principle applied equally to education as to the church: the
state ought not to interfere and provision of schools should be left
to individuals, societies and churches. When the need for State education became pressing, due to rapid population growth and the
inadequacy of private resources, Nonconformists came to accept the
idea of a state system, but insisted that the State was not competent
to give religious instruction. On this latter point Spurgeon expressed
his objection on three grounds: firstly, he personally disagreed with
much of the doctrine that would be taught; secondly, he believed that
doctrinal instruction would be used to reinforce the religious establishment; and thirdly, he doubted that religious instruction in schools
could ever be an effective influence to win the souls of children. But
Spurgeon would not accept 'banishing the Bible from the schools' altogether: a compromise was needed. In the end the Education Act
of 1870 included a provision which permitted local school boards to
include the Bible in the curriculum.

The Tory government of Benjamin Disraeli which took office in
early 1874 pursued a foreign policy which outraged Nonconformists,
and none more so than Spurgeon. The government's militaristic
stance gave rise to a popular feeling which became known as 'Jin-
goism' after the music hall song of 1878:

---

[7] *Sword and Trowel*, bound volume for 1867, p 516
[8] *Sword and Trowel*, bound volume for 1868, p 227

'We don't want to fight;
But by Jingo if we do,
We've got the ships,
We've got the men,
We've got the money too!'

As the nation embarked on more and more imperialistic ventures, in Afghanistan, South Africa and other places, Spurgeon was not afraid to express his forthright denunciation: 'We have invaded one country and then another with no better justification than the law of superior force, on the suspicion of future danger... We have meddled in many things, and have threatened at least three of the great quarters of the globe either with our fleets or our armies.' Spurgeon knew he was swimming against the tide of prevailing public opinion, which called for, in his words, '... a warlike policy as loudly as if it involved no slaughter, and were rather a boon to mankind than an unmitigated curse. A mysterious argument, founded upon the protection of certain mythical "British interests" is set up as an excuse, but the fact is that the national bulldog wants to fix his teeth into somebody's leg.'[9]

Spurgeon loathed war as much as Gladstone did. For him it was 'an unutterable evil, a curse to humanity, a pestilence to nations, and frequently an atrocity which excuses cannot palliate or eloquence conceal.'[10] First-hand experience with English soldiers during the Franco-Prussian War of 1870 left an indelible mark on Spurgeon's mind. In later years he did not share the public's near worship of General Gordon. He maintained that war was the product of sin and that it was only by God's intervention in human affairs that the world enjoyed any peace at all. He knew that if a society's warlike character were to change, it would be by individual transformation through the preaching of the gospel: 'All soul-saving', he argued, 'is a blow at the war-spirit.' The Christian '... becomes ashamed of blows and battles.' 'This peace-teaching', he continued, '... is but another name for practical gospel teaching.'[11]

Spurgeon saw the hand of God raised against the nation for its aggression and injustice abroad. As the Great Depression took hold and drought afflicted the country, he was convinced that it was the judgment of God:

---

[9] Article entitled 'Periodical War Madness' in *Sword and Trowel*, April 1878
[10] Article entitled 'Our Soldiers' in *Sword and Trowel*, March 1870
[11] *Periodical War Madness*, op cit

'We once hoped that peace was the favourite policy of England, but now Britannia thrusts her fists into everybody's face, and recklessly provokes hostility. The present ministry has sent the nation back half a century as to its moral tone; and it has laid up in the records of divine justice a sad amount of retribution, which is even now, in a measure, being meted out to the land ... It is our prayer that God may forgive the present belligerent ministers and either remove them from their offices or reverse their policy.'[12]

There were nevertheless justifications for war which Spurgeon held to, according to D N Duke[13]: firstly, because governments are God's instruments, and governments have deemed war necessary; secondly, because of sin, war will not cease until the reign of Christ with his Second Coming; thirdly, wars are permitted by God for necessary and useful purposes; fourthly, because war may be the last resort of an oppressed people.

Some Christians argued that the great expansion of Protestant missions owed much to military aggression opening up the way for heathen lands to receive the gospel. As early as 1854, Spurgeon strongly rejected the idea that the gospel could be spread by conquest: 'Whenever England goes to war, many shout, "It will open a way for the gospel." I cannot understand how the devil is to make a way for Christ; and what is war but an incarnate fiend, the impersonation of all that is hellish in fallen humanity ... For English cannon to make way for an English missionary is a lie too glaring for me to believe for a moment.'

When it came to the General Election of 1880, Spurgeon threw everything he had behind the Liberal cause. In his local constituency, Southwark, he publicly endorsed the two Liberal candidates. The subsequent Liberal victory in the seat was commonly attributed to Spurgeon's efforts, not least his posters attacking one of the Tory candidates for paying his workers paltry wages! Spurgeon was also busy in the neighbouring constituency, Lambeth, where, as 'your friend and neighbour, C H Spurgeon', he addressed the electors. The following is a convenient summary of his political views:

---

[12] *Sword and Trowel*, bound volume for 1879, p 245

[13] In his helpful article, 'Asking the Right Questions about War' in *Evangelical Quarterly*, vol LXI No.1 (January 1989)

'Do you sorrow over the warlike policy which has
thrust might into the place of right, and invaded weak nations with but scant excuse? Then return the two candidates who are opposed to the Beaconsfield ministry. Do
you believe that constant bluster creates political uneasi-
ness, and disturbs our peaceful relations with other nations, and thus hinders trade and commerce? then send
to Parliament Liberal candidates to strengthen the hands
of Mr Gladstone. Do you believe that great questions
of progress at home should no longer be pushed into a
corner? Then increase the number of men who are in
the advance guard of liberty. Lovers of religious equality, your course is plain ... With hands and heart support
the men who would rid religion of state patronage and
control. You who would ease the national burdens by
economy and retrenchment, vote for Messrs McArthur
and Lawrence ... Imagine another six years of Tory rule,
devoid alike of peace and progress, and you will rouse
yourself to do your duty ... '.[14]

To Spurgeon the religious beliefs, or lack of them, of any Parlia-
mentary candidate were immaterial as far as the electors' choice was
concerned. He defended the Mr Lawrence mentioned above when in
1868 the Tories accused him of heterodoxy. In 1880, against prevailing Nonconformist opinion, Spurgeon defended the right of Charles
Bradlaugh, a declared atheist, to take his seat in the House of Commons. For this he received the tribute from Annie Besant, writing in
the 'National Reformer', that he belonged to the order of '... Verta
brata, not to the mollusca.'

Loyal Liberal though he was, Spurgeon was more loyal to his
Lord. The issue of Home Rule for Ireland, which dominated the
latter part of Gladstone's career, highlighted Spurgeon's higher al-
legiance. He was passionately opposed to Home rule and felt that
Gladstone, who was equally passionate in the opposite direction, was
making an enormous mistake in proposing to grant self-government
to Ireland. With 80% of the population Roman Catholic, Home Rule
would be bound to produce in effect, Rome rule. Gladstone found
himself alienated from the Nonconformists on this issue, and indeed
from much of the Liberal party, whose radical wing was eager to get
on with pressing social reforms. Gladstone's obsession with Home

---

[14]Quoted in Kruppa, op cit

rule was a major contributing factor to the Liberals' loss of impetus at the end of the nineteenth century. They were unable to address the massive social changes which faced the country. People instead began to look to the emerging Labour movement to meet the challenge.

Spurgeon remained a 'Gladstonite' to the end. The divergence between the two men over Home Rule did not destroy a soul friendship.

That Spurgeon was a political force is abundantly clear. But what are we to make of his political involvement? What factors in him produced such a vigorous approach to issues of the day? There would seem to be five main features which underlie Spurgeon's approach to politics and call for our attention.

Firstly, he believed in a *full-orbed Christian morality*. Its searching demands embraced not only individual behaviour but the conduct of government policy towards other nations; not only the family but also the Cabinet.

Secondly, he believed in a *fully-sufficient gospel*. He urged men to come to Christ with utter conviction. When a man is saved, he becomes moral. Regarding drunkenness for example, Spurgeon says, 'The best way to make a man sober is to bring him to the foot of the cross.' Change in society for the better arises from a work of God accompanying the preaching of the biblical gospel in all its fullness.

Thirdly, he believed in *the vulnerability of the church* in this present age. Trials and struggles are normal. The Church must fight to make its voice heard. 'Truth is usually in the minority in this evil world', said Spurgeon at the time of the Downgrade controversy. Several years earlier, referring to 'ebbs and floods', he says: 'One day, "The kingdom of God suffereth violence, and every man presses into it"; at another time men seem to be ashamed of the Christian faith, and they wander off into a thousand delusions, and the church is minished and brought low by heresy, by worldliness, by lukewarmness, and by all sorts of evils.'[15]

Fourthly, he believed in *the rightness of influencing, not imposing*. The whole thrust of Spurgeon's political activity presumes this. He knew that the Church could not and should not seek to promote righteousness in the nation by forcibly imposing it through the agency of the State. He knew that the Church could not and should not assertively claim from God earthly superiority. Rather, the Church's

---

[15] *Metropolitan Tabernacle Pulpit*, 1882, p 110

function was to influence the government through legitimate protest and pressure; and to influence God by supplicatory and intercessory prayer to intervene for His glory.

Fifthly, he believed in *unqualified commitment to the Lord Jesus Christ.* Spurgeon regarded it as his duty and privilege to exhaust his life in the cause of his Saviour. Every faculty, every opportunity must be used. 'I feel that, if I could live a thousand lives, I would like to live them all for Christ, and I should even then feel that they were all too little a return for His great love to me.'[16]

---

[16] *Metropolitan Tabernacle Pulpit*, 1902, p 274

Publishers Note

Spurgeon loved the Puritans, and is considered by many to be "the last of the Puritans." In the collection at William Jewell College near Kansas City, Missouri, known as "the Spurgeon Collection," one will find Puritan tome after Puritan tome. Soli Deo Gloria has reprinted many classic and never-before-reprinted Puritan works. A partial list is provided below, many of which volumes are works that Spurgeon himself owned.

Adams, Thomas.	*A Commentary on 2 Peter*
Ainsworth, Henry.	*Annotation on the Pentateuch, Psalms, and Song of Solomon.* 2 volume set.
Binning, Hugh.	*The Works of Hugh Binning* in1 volume.
Bolton, Robert.	*General Directions for a Comfortable Walking with God* *A Treatise on Comforting Afflicted Consciences* *The Carnal Professor*
Bridge, William.	*The Works of William Bridge* in 5 volumes.
Burroughs, Jeremiah.	*The Saints' Happiness* *Gospel Fear* *Gospel Worship* *The Evil of Evils* *A Treatise of Earthly-Mndedness* *The Saints' Treasury*
Case, Thomas.	*The Select Works of Thomas Case*
Edwards, Jonathan.	*Selections from the Unpublished Writings*

Gray, Andrew.	*The Works of Andrew Gray* in 1 volume
Howe, John.	*The Works of John Howe* in 3 volumes
Jenkyn, William.	*An Exposition of the Epistle of Jude*
Mead, Matthew.	*The Almost Christian Discovered* *The Sermons of Matthew Mead*
Preston, John	*The Golden Sceptre*
Reynolds, Edward.	*The Sinfulness of Sin* (volume 1 of the works)
Shepard, Thomas	*The Works of Thomas Shepard* in 3 volumes
Stoddard, Solomon.	*A Guide to Christ*
Vincent, Thomas.	*The True Christian's Love to the Unseen Christ*
Watson, Thomas.	*Heaven Taken By Storm* *The Sermons of Thomas Watson* (Published in 1826 as "Discourses on Interesting and Important Subjects"
Compilation	*The Puritans on Conversion* (3 treatises by Samuel Bolton, Nathaniel Vincent, and Thomas Watson)
Compilation	*Farewell Sermons* (A collection of 23 sermons preached on the day of the Great Ejection in 1662)